BABIES ARE A LOT LIKE DRUNKS, NO MATTER HOW LATE IT IS IN THE NIGHT OR HOW EARLY IN THE MORNING BOTH WILL DEMAND THE BAR BE OPEN AND SCREAM AT YOU UNTIL IT IS.

Dedicated to

Louise, Lilly-Josephine and Huey

First published in the United Kingdom in 2016 by:

Lillypots Ltd
United Kingdom

For sales information or media enquiries please email
Becomingdaddy@lilly-pots.com

www.lilly-pots.com

 @lilly_pots   Lillypots

Front cover design: Back cover design:
Simone Hudson   Cain Lazenby
www.simoneamyhudson.com   www.nicheignite.com.au

Photography:
Hema Sabina   Telen Rodwell
www.Hemaphotography.com   www.Telenrodwell.com

Megan Bowen
www.snaplifephotography.com

Book design:
Studio Text
www.studiotext.co

ISBN 978-0-9954761-0-3

Printed by:
Hong Kong Magnetic Products Limited , Hong Kong

BECOMING DADDY

**There is no way to be a perfect Dad
but there are a million ways to be the best *one***

Tam Rodwell

Contents

The Introduction

I'll never forget the moment our front door closed behind us, and the sudden feeling of isolation that came over me. It was as if I had just been transported to the most remote planet in the universe. And I know Louise felt the same.

I know now that it's a very common feeling for all new parents when they leave the safe sanctuary of the hospital. Arriving home from hospital, only to realise they are truly on their own when the door shuts behind them, is terrifying. I thought I was prepared; I thought we were prepared, but the reality of it all was that no one had the slightest idea what to do. A few hours in, my wife was in tears. She just wanted to go back to the hospital, back to the safety of the doctors and midwives and high-tech medical equipment.

To be fair, I was also quite ready to pack up the three of us and drive back to the hospital, and once there, I would have begged for re-admittance. We were just not ready! And, most certainly, we were a danger to our newborn baby. How could the hospital staff possibly have let us leave the hospital with this tiny newly born person? Surely they'd made a mistake! We must have slipped out, unnoticed, through some "parenting turnstile" that vets whether parents are actually qualified or not. How could they possibly have let us leave? How could they?

All I can really remember through those first few hours after the birth is the constant, soothing talk of Cleo. Cleo was our supervising midwife after Lilly-Jo was delivered. She made us feel safe, while at the same time teaching us how to care for our newborn infant. Cleo was one of those warm and cuddly types. She could do no wrong. I'm fairly sure that given the choice of taking me and the baby, or Cleo and the baby, back home with her, my wife would have left me sitting in the waiting room; without so much as a second thought!

Slowly the hours passed and those hours turned into days and at last we both felt as if we were, slowly, heading back through the Universe towards Earth. We were fortunate to have a grandmother to help us in those first few months and I think she was ultimately our baby saviour. When I look back on the last few years, it's hard to place anything in any kind of order. It all seems to be melded together in this epic blur of life, where experiences and feelings continue to constantly flash before my eyes.

All I can tell you is that I did my best and l learned a heck of a lot along the way. While I'm far from the perfect husband or dad, I did things in my own crazy way and I made sure everyone around me was looked after, the best I could. I never wanted to be the kind of dad who had to ask my wife what time of day the babies need to eat, or what time they sleep during the day and for how long. I felt I should know. It became simpler when I realized I did know, and it was easy to do; by paying attention and spending as much time with my wife and babies that I could. I knew what to do because I had invested my heart, soul, and my time in them as much and as often as possible.

There is almost nothing you learn about your own child or how your partner feels by reading a book or researching online.

As I begin to write about my experiences and share them here, I realise I never wanted this to be a manual on how to be a great dad. All I want is to share my experiences in a fun and interesting way. I hope that it helps someone out there who struggled just like I did at times.

I wish all you new dads out there the best of luck and good fortune! The adventure of a lifetime is just beginning.

Tam Rodwell

How To Build A Super Baby

Even the pasta was cooked in broccoli water.

There aren't going to be many chapters in this book where I get on my soapbox. I promised myself that. This chapter, however, is probably going to be one of them. If you're reading this now and you have just discovered you're going to be a dad, the following few paragraphs might be the most important you ever read. Let's talk about pregnant women and eating!

Every time your partner eats during her pregnancy it's a golden opportunity to provide top quality nutrition to her and your developing little one. Don't be foolish and try kidding yourself that a healthy and properly developed baby is all down to chance and the genetic lottery. Sure, they are major factors, but remember you are starting from scratch here and literally growing a human that begins with a tiny embryo. It's amazing! Every single thing your partner eats will also go to the baby and each tiny morsel of nutrition will be building them, one block at a time.

FRUITS, VEGETABLES AND PROTEIN – Think about it.

I'm certainly no dietician, but it's commonly said that fruits, vegetables and protein are very important for your pregnant partner to eat regularly. Make it a point to try each day to be responsible getting one nutritious meal into your partner. That's simple isn't it? If you can do this every day then you will have played a major role in how your baby develops. You see, this eating and nutrition game is pretty much down to you, and only you, at many points throughout the pregnancy. Women can get incredibly tired during these nine months. They don't have energy to cook nutritious meals by day's end. I'd often come home and find Louise passed out cold, face down at the table, curled up on a chair or collapsed on the sofa where she'd clearly dropped on the way to doing something. It's often hard for mums-to-be, and mums, to be able to summon the energy to cook a balanced meal. This is where you can (and need to) step up and take charge. For certain, taking charge will be a relief for your partner.

There are so many things you can do to help her eat a decent meal full of the things both she and a growing baby need. It's as easy as making a packed lunch for work or making a little extra at dinner and freezing portions that she can reheat later. Always have a ready supply of fruit and healthy snacks and always text her on your way home from work. She may need something but she will love that you want to know if there is anything she particularly fancies. Pregnant women's cravings change like the wind and it's a small thing you can do. You'll really need to have your A Game on to keep up with them.

I have to say that pregnancy and eating can also be a frustrating time for dads-to-be. Women often suffer periods of morning sickness, which can really put them off food. I can remember a time when all Louise would eat was "anything white" i.e. bread, plain pasta, and rice. I was running around, thinking that this baby is going to have malnutrition. I even started doing sneaky things like boiling pasta and noodles in fresh vegetable broth, hoping that would add a small amount of nutrition.

Pregnancy was something I never really tried to understand. It was more of a thing I tried to help with. I was putting in the effort to raise a healthy child, even before she was born. As I found out later, it's a lot easier to get an unborn child to eat broccoli than a screaming one sitting in a high chair.

But that's something you'll probably discover for yourself very soon.

The Car Seat Test

*That box has the potential to be
full of ridicule, lots of ridicule.*

I can remember a few years back when Prince George was born in London and how all the excitement had gripped the UK. My wife and mother-in-law were glued to the TV, trying to catch a glimpse of the Royal Baby, as William and Kate left the hospital. I remember watching William bring George out, in his car seat, and place him seamlessly into the waiting car. Most people probably wouldn't have noticed how impressive it was but I turned to Louise straight-away and said, 'He's been practising that!' I was rather pleased with myself and, I admit, a bit smug, for knowing this.

You see, the car seat test with your newborn baby is one of the toughest you will face in the first few days of your new life as a dad. Your victorious, or failed attempts will most likely be played out to a gallery of family and judgemental relatives. Trust me, history is lit-tered with broken dads, following their attempts to safely get baby from the hospital car park to the front door of their house.

If you're expecting a baby any time soon you should have pur-chased a car seat by now. I recommend getting one around halfway through that nine-month period. I can't stress how important it is to take the time to research and find out which seat is best for you and your needs. Until we purchased ours, I assumed that these seats were pretty much all the same. I also wrongly assumed that they would be easy to figure out. While I won't say they are the most complicated things you'll put together, there are still a few complexities to navigate. I found the actual straps that bind the baby are a little confusing. Yes, simple straps were confusing.

If you want my advice on types to buy, I'd say choose one that has a fixed base that stays permanently in your car. All you'll then have to do is strap baby in and click the seat in or out of the car. No messing with seat belt straps. This is particularly useful when little humans fall asleep while you're driving. With luck and practice, when the time comes that you have to move them inside, you can move the sleeping kiddo in without too much noise when you arrive at your destination.

To be honest, though, there is little use in my going into great detail about how to fix a car seat, as I've only fitted two. There are hundreds of different types out there. This book isn't really about solving problems for you; rather it's about helping you identify things that you need to resolve yourself because that's the best way to learn.

I actually asked my own dad about his experiences and he said that back in the seventies, they took me home from the hospital in a bassinet that was strapped into the back seat of their borrowed Mini Cooper S. Now that doesn't really sound too bad until I tell you that it was strapped in with rope. Oh, the shuddering about the health and safety practices of our beloved ancestors. To continue on with amusing anecdotes, here is a short list of things that every new parent should know before leaving hospital...

FIVE THINGS EVERY NEW PARENT SHOULD KNOW BEFORE LEAVING HOSPITAL WITH THEIR BABY

1. Everything will seem a lot louder than when you arrived in the delivery room! Birds chirping, dogs barking, people sneezing! They're all involved in a huge conspiracy to wake your baby.

2. Driving home with your baby will feel like your first driving test. The steering wheel will feel heavy and you'll check every mirror at least once every five seconds. You will indicate so early for a turn that other drivers, who, of course are trying to maim you, will overtake you before you even get there.

3. Simple things like crossing the road will suddenly feel like a trip down white water rapids. Driverless cars, reckless skateboarders and rogue boulders are, of course, all out to mow your family down.

4. No matter how much of a party animal you were or how many all-nighters you pulled at work before, nothing can quite prepare you for spending all night with a crying infant. Every new parent will, at some point, pay $1000 for five minutes sleep.

5. Visitors will inundate you and your family. It will start at the hospital and continue in your living room. They will arrive bearing all sorts of impractical gifts, like flowers or scented candles. You won't even have the chance to wonder if a pizza might arrive. You will be too busy making them cups of tea.

So, dads-to-be, as far as the safety of your new baby, and getting yourself a car seat is concerned, it's time to get proactive. If you leave this box unticked, I promise you it will lead to much stress, and possibly a bit of humiliation on your part.

I've actually seen dads in hospital car parks trying to erratically fit these things, and I do believe my best friend's father actually turned up with one, still in its box! It's crazy, really, that men want to put themselves through this. The whole process of childbirth, while amazing, is also very emotionally and physically draining for both parties. You will walk out of that hospital with your head spinning and I am telling you now that you need to know that the very first task of securing the car seat should already be second nature. It's an easy win, don't waste it.

Hopefully this has scared you enough to take the car seat issue seriously. If not, your failed attempts will more than likely be cannon fodder over many Xmas dinners, birthdays and weddings to come. I warned you. You're welcome!

Need help?
incarsafetycentre.co.uk

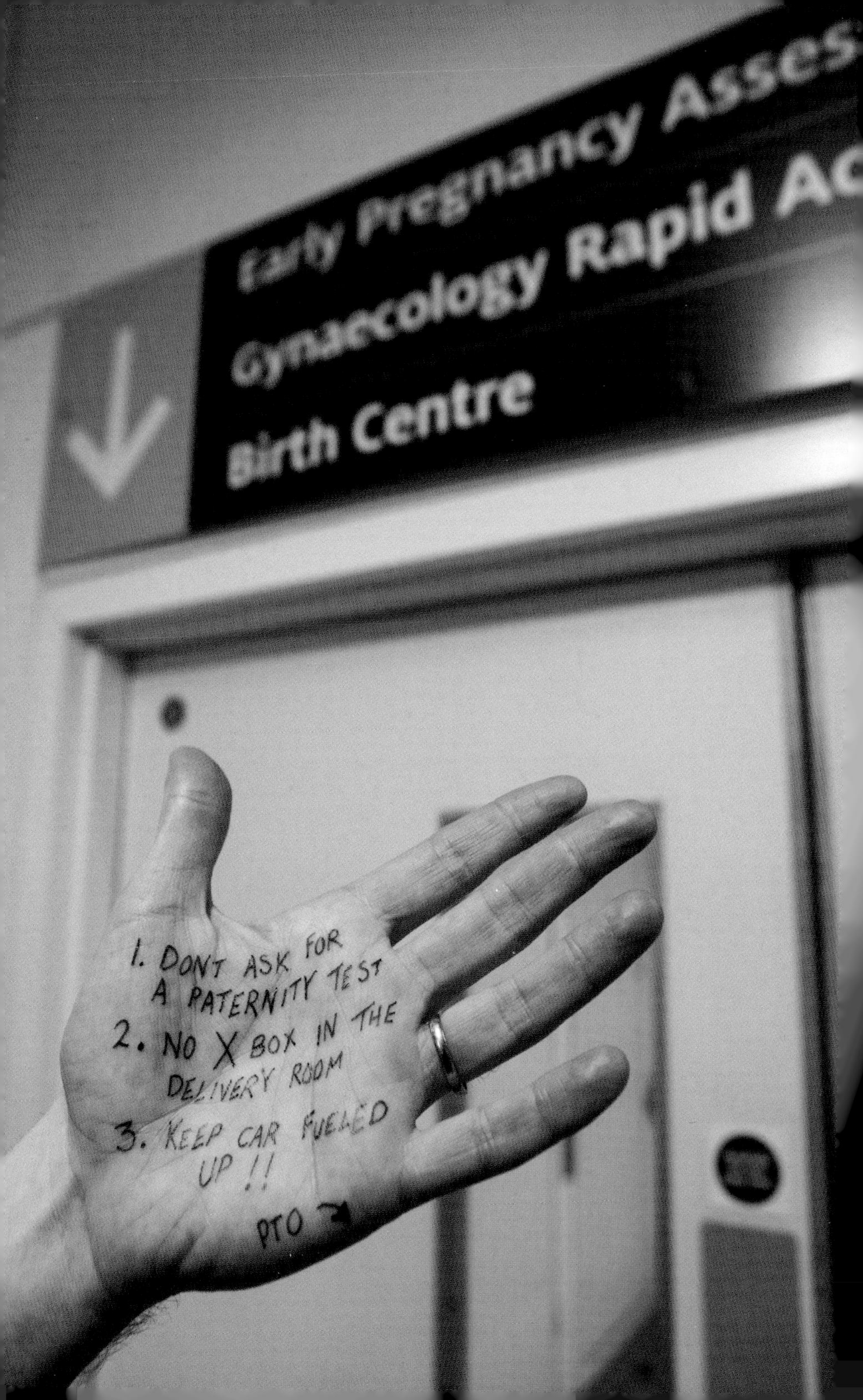
Early Pregnancy Asses
Gynaecology Rapid Ac
Birth Centre
1. DONT ASK FOR A PATERNITY TEST
2. NO X BOX IN THE DELIVERY ROOM
3. KEEP CAR FUELED UP !!
PTO

The Big Day

Even after plan B has failed, there are still another 24 letters in the alphabet to use to plan for the arrival of your baby.

I actually decided not to do a chapter on the ins and outs of the hospital delivery room (sorry I just couldn't resist that one!). The birth of your baby is such an amazing personal moment that I think every father should enjoy it on their own terms, without any expectations or interferences from others. Like the many things I've written about in this book, a lot of the stress and worry in most situations can be taken out of the equation just by simple planning and being prepared. It's far more useful to immerse yourself in the preparation for your partner's due date than to worry about the day itself. As you'll discover, the actual events of the day will simply take care of themselves.

One of the first opportunities to show your support is by attending your partner's doctor's appointments and ultrasounds. There will be quite a number of doctor's appointments and it isn't essential that you attend all of them. It's difficult sometimes with work commitments and other obligations, so talk it over with your partner and see which appointments she would like you to attend. As far as the ultrasounds go, I don't think you really have a clause to opt out here and if you're anything like me, you'll be well up for going along and seeing the first glimpses of your handiwork. Ultrasound appointments are usually very pleasant experiences and it's a little like going to the movies knowing that what you're about to see will be your favourite movie of all time until the day you die.

I also really wanted to talk specifically about antenatal (Lamaze) classes, as it's more than likely you'll be attending them. We enjoyed ours very much, although I will say there wasn't a great deal I remembered that I actually used in practice. It was comforting that at least I tried to prepare myself for the big day. Probably the highlight for me was learning how to change a diaper, albeit on a plastic doll. There are very few times in life you'll get to practise changing a diaper before you actually need to, so appreciate it as it will be the easiest and the least toxic one you'll ever change. More than anything, antenatal classes were a chance to bond with other parents, eat biscuits and let the mums-to-be talk about how much they miss drinking wine. So don't be expecting too much, just go and have fun. If I had my chance to do it again, I wouldn't have been so serious about it.

If you're lucky enough to be living in the UK then you'll be in good hands as the National Childbirth Trust (NCT) runs a very good programme for parents-to-be, and I couldn't recommend it more highly. While I've got you here, be sure to look into hiring a *TENS* machine for your partner even if you never use it. A *TENS* machine is a device that looks a bit like a TV remote control and has wires coming out of it, with adhesive pads that emit an electric current. It's very useful for when your partner starts to get a bit hysterical; you can just zap her, much like using a *Taser* gun. No! No! Of course it doesn't work like that. *TENS* machines are an excellent way to help your partner get through the pain of contractions and I'd highly recommend you hire one. This is one you will really, really (really!) need to learn how to use first, so don't you dare leave it sitting in the box until it's too late! Get it out, read the instructions and have a trial run. The small adhesive pads for the calming current fix to her back, so only you can attach it for her. While I'm on contractions, be sure to also download an app that can time hers when she goes into labour. At some point you'll have to call a hospital and one of the main things they will want to know is how far apart the contractions are. In this day and age almost everyone has a smart phone and little things like this are invaluable. When she starts to go into labour you'll forget your ABCs, let alone know how to count.

As you know, I've already devoted an entire chapter to purchasing a car seat but it's also worth mentioning how important it is to have an adequate amount of fuel in the car. Imagine what would happen if you ran out of petrol and were stranded on the side of the highway. Are you capable of delivering a baby? It may sound stupid but please be sure that you also know the route to the hospital, especially if you are visiting a different town or city. I know these two things seem like common sense but you'd be surprised how many dads get caught out, and, as I said earlier, there just isn't any need to. Basic preparation can avoid the stress in all of these situations. That now brings me to the concept of discussing a birth plan with your partner. Relatively simple, a birth plan basically outlines ideas you would both have regarding how you want the birth to go. Considerations such as...

1. Does she want to have a water birth or drug free birth?
2. Who do you want in the delivery room with you?
3. How will you announce the birth to family and friends?

I also really think it's important to have a birth plan ready just in case something does go wrong. If mother and baby have to be separated after the birth for any reason, you need to know what her wishes are. I would expect that she will want you to go with your baby, so it's probably a good idea to have someone who can step in and look after your partner in your absence. Birth plans are not so much about following a plan but sitting down with your loved one and listening to her. She will be scared. All women are, at least a little bit, when it comes to childbirth and it's an excellent way to show your support. Be the partner who suggests that you sit down and do this. Take charge and let her know you're there for her.

Ultimately, what you will find with the birth is that none of it will go exactly to plan. However there might just be one or two little things that you follow that will make all the difference.

It's also important that you have a few things packed yourself for the hospital visit as you will more than likely be there for some time. You don't have to go too crazy but at least have a nice change of clothes to leave the hospital with. I took a fresh pair of jeans as well as a t shirt and a pair of socks, and it was nice to walk out of the hospital not looking like the emotional (but happy) wreck I felt like. I further advise you to have a few basic toiletry items with you as well, such as a toothbrush and deodorant. You're going to be up close and personal with her in the delivery room so keep it fresh. You should also definitely pack a phone charger! It's estimated on average that new parents take nine hundred and fifty photos of their newborn baby in the first three minutes of life, so it's essential to have an adequate charging facility!

However, don't sweat it. If you do forget anything most hospitals are usually fairly close to all sorts of shops etc. I doubt there's much you couldn't pop out and get, if need be.

The only other thing worth mentioning is perhaps getting your partner a little gift for her efforts giving birth. They call these gifts "push" presents and can be given before or after the birth. I won't lie to you. I didn't get Louise anything when Lilly-Jo was born as I just thought it was another one of these commercial gimmicks. I'd been tremendously supportive anyway so nothing else was needed. However, once you actually witness childbirth, you'll probably be rushing out to buy whatever you can when you know the second baby is on the way. Nothing overly expensive is required; something like a nice bracelet, a gift voucher to her favourite shop, or some chocolates. It's really more about the thought with "push" presents rather than the gift itself.

So there you have it. This was a pretty basic guide to preparing for the birth of your baby. Even if you only follow some of the ideas, it's better than nothing. Again, the whole experience should be as you and your partner want it. So, as long as you both enjoy it, don't worry too much about things and enjoy the moment.

The Visitors

*Shut the blinds, lock the door
and don't make a sound.*

It begins when they start arriving at the hospital and quickly moves on to your living room, where they will also be waiting. With arms outstretched and eyes round like saucers, they will be exploding with delirium and desperately hoping to get some face time with your newborn baby. We are, of course, talking about the visitors you will be inundated with shortly after the arrival of your bundle of joy.

I'm a firm believer that newborn babies emit some kind of youthful essence that is apparently irresistible to family and friends. This invisible essence is also particularly alluring to the elderly, especially if it's your first baby. They'll flock from far and wide to coo and fuss. There will be the devouring of cakes and tea, none of which they will have brought and none you'll ever see again, as they vanish into the abyss of a crazed Mad Hatter's tea party.

Of course I'm not being totally serious...not totally. We are blessed to have a wonderfully supportive family network but it is always amusing to poke fun at how crazy they all become when baby visitation rights are finally granted. I wasn't joking about the elderly, though. They can suddenly go from slightly immobile to superhuman when a new baby is involved. Take Lilly-Jo and Huey's Great Grandparents, for example. They may be a little under the

weather and housebound for the last week but if a cuddle with a newborn is on the cards, they'll be bouncing around like shiny new springs. Not only will they arrive in their Sunday best but they will do it all without the need for a SATNAV. Guided by the essence of your baby, they'll know instinctively the shortest route between their driveway and your house.

Kidding aside, it is a tricky time for new parents in the first few weeks after the birth and it can be very overwhelming when there is a procession of visitors arriving at your house. I highly recommend you and your partner have a discussion about how you are going to deal with crowd control, as you are the only ones who can. I would love to say that as the man of the house, you will have equal say on what happens over this visitation period, but if your house is anything like mine, then it's usually the women folk who have the deciding vote. This imbalance has been going on for millennia and no sane man would dare challenge this. I'm no different.

I'm of the strong opinion that there should be some kind of universal manual you can hand out to loved ones. It would make things easier as it would set them clear guidelines for visits and also, spell out the do's and don'ts of visiting a newborn's house. There is very little self-regulation when it comes to visiting a baby during the newborn period. If you're feeling like you just can't deal with it, pick a trusted family member or friend to do the organising/herding for you.

I have to say that after the birth, friends and family should be invited to the hospital to fawn and fuss but then after that, the family should be left for two weeks at home alone to adjust to their new life. Of course that was never going to happen but that was what I suggested and I'm sure at some point during the visitor chaos, that Louise did consider it. We do occasionally butt heads a bit on affairs of this matter but generally we meet in the middle somewhere and that's how a good marriage should work.

My wife, you see, is one of those amazing hostesses. I remember a few weeks after Lilly-Jo was born she announced we were having a brunch for close family and that I would be in charge of cooking for everyone. It was indeed a lavish affair with all sorts of balloons and bunting adorning the walls. Guests enjoyed endless refills of tea and the baby was passed from one lap to the next for hours on end. I don't doubt that everyone had a lovely time but people really just came to see the baby. I remember saying to Louise later that I felt she tries to over-do things at times and that she shouldn't trouble herself because no one really expected her to do anything like what they got that day. I doubt any of them would have complained if I downed tools and went upstairs for a nap instead. In fact, I am quite sure no one remembered that she and I were even in the room!

However, what you have to understand, I suppose, is that your partner has carried this baby for nine months in trying times so she does get to decide how things go down. Please try not to be such a wet blanket like me. You may by default, end up being that wet blanket because no matter what, you will experience visitors who are less than helpful. I try not to worry about it too much as I think the euphoria of a new baby can sometimes cloud people's heads.

In that vein, a good guest should intend to come for no more than an hour, and this visit should start at a specified time. There is nothing worse than you changing baby into a nice outfit and having them fed and ready, only for your guest to arrive half an hour late. By that stage the baby probably needs feeding again and has thrown up all over that new outfit and is now back in their PJs. The circle can be very tiring!

It's this sort of visitor, the one who has not a clue about what's good for the new family, which new parents can do without! There is no such thing as fashionably late when it comes to visiting a new family if the visit is at 12pm. A visitor should arrive at 12pm. I would like to add however, that if you're fortunate like us, you will be blessed with some truly lovely guests. These kinds of guests may bring food over flowers and instead of obsessing over the new baby, they take your older child and play with them instead. I'm more than happy to double the allocated visiting slot for people such as this, as they have shown a true understanding of what is required.

That said, in my ideal world, everyone would bring a nice pizza when they come. While flowers are lovely they certainly don't taste like pepperoni and we only have a limited amount of vases in the house. So if you're a guest, and you see your flowers propped up in a Tupperware box then it's probably time to have a rethink about your chosen gift.

So there you have an idea of what can happen socially post-birth. Remember, you hold the trump card (the baby) and don't ever be afraid to say enough is enough. Over-extending yourself and getting all the more tired won't do anyone any good, least of all your baby. Let your visitors know politely when you are tired and suggest that they might like to keep their visit brief. If you do at least some of these things, I promise the first few weeks will be easier and less chaotic. Good luck!

Bringing Huey home
from hospital.

My Biggest Fear

I'm not scared of death, I'm scared of leaving them alone in the world.

Sometimes the things we don't talk about are the things that matter most.

When you're a young man, you don't really stop to consider your own mortality, and that's the way it should be. In our youth, old age and the possibility of death just seems like such a massive distance away that the whole concept seems impossible. I remember when I was barely out of my teens there was an American show on TV in Australia called *Thirty Something*. I don't think it was all that popular, and probably didn't last more than a season, but I watched it a few times. It was a bit of a *Friends* type of show but instead of comedy, it dealt with the angst of thirtysomethings as they catapulted from one disastrous relationship crisis to the next. It used to always make me laugh, as thirty-five seemed so old. I was sure I was never going to be that old, or that pathetic. While I don't think I ever became pathetic I certainly did become old and now, I'm probably five years the senior of those characters that I so openly mocked.

Old Man Time sneaks up on us all, for better or worse, but I'm feeling a slight shift for myself as my own mortality appears not quite the distant laughable affair that it was way back then. Until recently I never really felt any fear of death, and I'm quite comfortable in saying that as it's not a "macho" guy thing or any-thing like that. While I certainly wouldn't want to leave the world in a horrible, violent way, I've always been fairly comfortable believing that when the powers that be decide your number is up, then it's up. Even when Lilly-Jo was younger, I really felt the same. It may sound cold and uncaring in a way but having kids didn't suddenly fill within me a desire to live forever to protect them; and I am a doting, very caring dad. I think there's a difference in being a very protective father and also wanting an eternal life in order to always watch over your children.

That all changed in the last few months and it's hard for me to really pin point why that was. I think it was partially because one day I looked up at Lilly-Jo and realised she wasn't a baby anymore. It's not that I hadn't been paying attention, but all of a sudden she had become this amazing little person with her own very strong personality. It was the first time I was able to imagine her being grown up. When your little ones are small it's impossible to think that they will ever be grown up and living in the big bad world; maybe even without you. I was suddenly and inexplicably struck with a fear of death and the possibility of leaving them alone and abandoned in the world.

I've lived a pretty full life and while I've seen and experienced some amazing moments, I've also seen the very ugly side that life has to offer. Things aren't always nice. People are not always nice, and now all of a sudden I realised that Lilly-Jo, and now our new baby boy, would have to one day walk through this world alone. I guess I see a huge contrast in how the world is now for kids com-pared to what it was when I was growing up. We all know that the family unit as a whole isn't what it used to be, and I guess the trick-le-down effect is that a lot of the youth of today is disenchanted at not having the stability of family. When we think about the words, "the haves and the have-nots" we usually correlate this with wealth. But for me the wealth factor is not really what it's about. Kids that think bullying is normal or that violence is just part of getting what you want; these are the things that I dread every day and I can honestly say I just don't know how to prepare my kids for the reality of all of that.

I worry that Lilly-Jo and Huey are going to grow up alongside other kids who, by no fault of their own, didn't have the upbringing that I feel they should have. Kids who maybe don't have a mum or a dad or never had enough time spent with them, teaching them basic skills about how to treat others. That's not to say that you can't raise perfect children as a single parent; of course you can. It's really about how much time the parent(s) invest in their kids that make better or worse people, for lack of a better explanation.

Louise and I often have a slight conflict from time to time about the best way to raise our kids. I think she, like all mums, wants to keep them safe from danger, even if that means cocooning them a little more than she should. I honestly don't blame her at all as she is a fantastic mother, but I think they should be exposed to the big wide world, warts and all, to make it easier for them to survive it as wiser people. One example (maybe strange to you) of our varying parental ideas can be seen when Lilly-Jo was ready for the pool and swimming. I insisted I wanted to gently immerse her underwater, just to get her used to actually being underwater. It was just a simple thing, or so I thought. Louise was having none of this, as she was sure she'd drown. We went back and forth a bit but in the end, she won and Lilly-Jo's hair remained dry. Although I can see where she was coming from, we just disagreed on the best way to make Lilly-Jo water savvy.

There is a bit of a hidden analogy about life in that story, about how we both differ slightly on our parenting styles. I'm sure you'll experience your own ones. You need to work together to best prepare your kids for the real world. You really don't have as long as you think you do.

I'm also aware that at certain times, there are different ways that a mother and father express their protective instincts. While I can't comment on women specifically, I feel often that the pressures of keeping a child safe can be a very mentally draining experience. For me personally, it's not so much the fear of something bad happening to my wife and children, but more the fear of not being there to protect them if it does. I'm not sure how I would deal with a situation like that if it did occur. At times men can be accused of not showing they care enough but believe me, it's there, and the fear is in us too; we just don't like to show it. This is a good point to talk about with your partner if you ever run into one of those conversations where you're accused of not showing enough of a particular kind of emotion. Women need to understand that men feel emotions just as much as they do, but we are not genetically wired to be able to process them. Also, many men are brought up to believe that showing emotions is akin to weakness. Sometimes in this regard it really can be a case of "dammed if you do and damned if you don't". My feelings about my own mortality have changed because I'm in a different position than I have been in the past. I do certainly feel a sense that it's suddenly more important that I look after myself and be in a decent mental and physical state so I am able to watch over my little ones. At the same time, I don't want to wrap them in cotton wool, and my goal is still the same in that I want them to be wise to the ways of the world.

Much to the astonishment of those around me, I recently decided to take an extended break from beer, which up until now has been a big part of who I am. I'm actually a pretty sensible drinker but there's no denying I do love it a bit too much. I had managed to give up smoking about eleven years ago, and I thought it was at least time to test my will-power with alcohol. Although I felt fine and beer wasn't making me physically unwell, I guess you have to be realistic when you hit forty and start looking after yourself better. I've managed 9 months so far, and while I'm not planning on being teetotal forever, it's been nice to shift another vice for a little while.

Maybe I just needed to feel the fear of death to balance out my life a little? I'm not sure. They do say that fatherhood can creep up on a man. One day you're single and carefree and the next you look up and there is a wife and two kids! Where the heck did they come from? They weren't there last time I looked, or something to that effect. For me, certain things did definitely creep up. Everyone comes to their own realisations in life at their own speed, but I'm certainly glad it came sooner rather than later.

My biggest fear, while at times unpleasant, has also given me new drive to be an even better dad than I thought I could be and to ensure that Lilly-Jo and Huey are ready for the world; and that I'm here to watch over them as long as I can.

How To Be A
Better Husband

*Try not to be too smug, dear.
All the other mums will hate you.*

Empathy: understanding another person's condition from their perspective.

Place yourself in their shoes and feel what they are feeling.

So let's talk about empathy and how important it is, especially when your partner is pregnant. Since we can't be the ones who are pregnant, I wanted to share my philosophy on how I tackled pregnancy with understanding. Do you usually leave your towel on the bathroom floor in the morning and your dirty socks "anywhere"?

Think again! Go around the house holding a 20lb bag of potatoes (your pretend baby) and try and pick up and wash all of that stuff and see how you feel!

Then for good measure try and pretend that the bag of potatoes is crying uncontrollably, and possibly peeing/being sick as well, and then you might think twice about it. What's the moral of the story, you might wonder? Well, here is my version and how empathy is key to getting through the earliest parts of parenthood...

I really tried to be as empathic as I could during my wife's pregnancy. You may snicker at that and maybe you'd be right to. I mean, how can you, as a man, even begin to put yourself into the shoes (or body) of a pregnant woman? And let's be honest, if given the opportunity to carry a child, would you want to? Think about that for a moment and then embrace empathy! By now you know that I tried hard to be very understanding during Louise's time when she was carrying our little ones, as well as when they were newly born and she was home all day with them. Looking back a bit, I can tell you that pregnancy is something that we dads will never really understand. It certainly doesn't hurt to try, though. I do believe the harder you try to help her through it, especially if it's her first time, the more you will be rewarded with her respect in the future.

First of all, dads-to-be, the most important thing you need to appreciate is that pregnancy is incredibly tiring, especially during the first three months. Smoother sailing happens mid-pregnancy but tiredness and stress come back stronger right at the end when she is feeling totally immobile, overwhelmed and just wanting it to be over. In the early stages of pregnancy, when her body is going through so many rapid changes and so much upheaval, fatigue is so great that just keeping her eyes open is all but impossible. Louise used to describe the feeling of tiredness like trying to wade through quicksand whilst also under water. She said, for her, it was a kind of tiredness that no amount of sleep could fix. These things she said, really made me try and be more aware of how much I needed to do to help her throughout those nine months.

Remember, everything is amplified during pregnancy. Everything! The good things she is feeling, like the feeling of baby's first hiccups or tiny first-kicks in her tummy, create unimaginable highs. The bad things, however, can be very high too! She could be very emotional, or she would have unexplainable aches and pains all over.

Pregnancy is really like riding a roller coaster of emotions and aches and pains, complete with thrills and excitement too, all while holding onto a sack of potatoes.

This is exactly my point and why I'm using a bag of potatoes for this chapter. The good and the bad of it all become even stranger and more intense when a sack of potatoes enters every aspect of your life. Small messes and specks of dirt can explode into World War 3. If you were thinking about going to bed and leaving your dirty dishes on the sink for later, think again. New mums hate messes. They create enough of it, by default, so they certainly don't need any extra from you.

Pregnancy and coping with a newborn are fleeting moments in time and will be over before you know it. Forget about your needs for a while. You've got plenty of great stuff to look forward to and nothing beats the relief that a wife or partner experiences knowing that daddy is in charge of the family's happiness and cleanliness. It makes you feel full of pride and satisfaction too!

The Breastfeeding Journey

Welcome to Boobtown: Population 2

Breastfeeding is an uncomfortable topic for some men, and that's fine. I'm certainly not here to convince you whether it's right for you and your family. However, I'm being totally unapologetic for raising the issue, as I am a very enthusiastic supporter of my wife's attempts to breastfeed our children. She put in a stellar effort for seven months with our firstborn, Lilly-Jo and even donated her extra breastmilk for the Prem babies at the local hospital. We rarely used formula until she was weaned and we are proud of being able to do this for as long as we did. At present Louise is nursing our new baby boy, Huey.

There is a wealth of information out there about the benefits of breastfeeding. You should read it and make your own judgement. Any life decision should be based on knowledge instead of misconceptions. You can't even begin to imagine the misunderstandings, falsehoods and inaccuracies about breastfeeding. Use the information out there to really learn all you can, because the choice of whether to breastfeed or not is very important. Luckily, here in the United Kingdom, our National Health Service is pro-breast-feeding and that's incredibly helpful. But as grateful as we were for the support made available, I made a decision that my wife needed some extra support.

Learning to breastfeed is sometimes hard. Breastfeeding doesn't always come naturally just because you've given birth. You may not know this but there are babies who don't know how to breastfeed either. The skill to successful breastfeeding has many different elements and many mums have told me the reason they failed with breastfeeding was because they didn't get enough support and information. In other words, they didn't fail because they couldn't do it. I liken breastfeeding to trying to learn complicated algorithms, immediately following a traffic accident.

When Lilly-Jo was a few weeks old, I paid for a private expert to come to our house to help Louise with some of her breastfeeding issues. The money I spent on the consultation worked wonders and totally transformed Louise's technique. You may not need to hire an expert though, so be sure to ask your local health office about resources available to you and your family.

One thing I do want you to be aware of is the sheer amount of time breastfeeding can take. Babies sometimes "cluster feed" in their early stages. This is when they take small amounts of milk with short breaks in between. Cluster feeding happens because a baby's stomach is so tiny that it can only process small amounts of food. Look at a baby's fist; this is the size of baby's tummy! That's not very big at all. When it comes to feeding, babies stop and start a lot (like traffic, if you will) and this can go on and on and on…for hours. I'm serious. Once you know this and are prepared for it though, it won't be too bad. Imagine how you and your breastfeeding partner would feel not knowing this; you'd probably be thinking your baby isn't getting enough to eat or that you're not doing it "right". For once, you'd actually be wrong—and that would be good!

Be prepared for the large amounts of nothing that mum will get done. Normal things like eating and going to the bathroom will seem like mirages in the desert. If you suddenly realise that this is occurring, you can bet that she needs rest—desperately. Keep a watch out but don't try to give her a break by taking the baby for a while. Taking the baby "off her hands" can seem like a good solution, but it may cause both her and the baby more stress to be apart (even if they seem calm), which will detract from their rest. A better solution is to take care of everything else around the house. Do something simple like making your bed as safe as possible so she and the baby can lie down to nurse and doze. However, once feeding time is over then mum will greatly appreciate your taking baby so she can have a little break.

Little ones can be quite diligent workers (feeders) at times, and it would be nothing to see them feeding on and off for five hours straight, just when you thought they had a "schedule". At this point, any plans you have will be meaningless if baby decides it's time for a marathon-style feeding session. All you can do is sit and wait patiently. Getting stressed out isn't doing anyone any favours. It's not wise to become agitated when you aren't keeping to your schedule. In fact, you may want to just forget your schedule for a few months!

One of the difficulties with breastfeeding is that it gets in the way of your togetherness. During this time, you might feel neglected when it comes to getting attention from your wife. A lot of men find this hard, and I know I had my moments. We are only human and it's a big adjustment starting a new life with little babies. I promise you, things will return to normal but it will take time. You can help speed this up by being as supportive as possible and trying to remain close. There is a little known fact that may help you sneak in some rest and relaxation, mother's milk delivers sleep! Breast milk contains a naturally occurring type of morphine (well not really morphine—but it is like a powerful sleep drug) that can knock babies out cold. Some even call babies "milk drunk" after they have had a feed and have gone straight to sleep. The more you give them, the better they will sleep. And the more they sleep, the more we sleep...Are you following here?

As always though, it pays to ask questions as much as you can, so don't be shy when you're in the hospital for the birth, and during your aftercare. Here are my top tips to help you help your partner breastfeed your new baby.

- Pay attention to the midwives when they are assisting your wife after delivery. It's all about getting the baby to latch on correctly. You really need to understand the mechanics of it all, for lack of a better word

- Consider buying a proper feeding pillow for her—it made a huge difference for us. Also, don't forget to buy a tube of Lanolin cream—it's essential for when certain parts of her body start to get a little sore from the suckling

- When you control the food, you control the mood! Be prepared to help your partner eat while she's feeding the baby. I spent many a night cutting up Louise's dinner and feeding her with a fork. It is one of my fondest moments—the daisy chain of helpless people feeding each other

- Keeping hydrated comes first! Feeding mums can get ridiculously thirsty. Make sure there is always a full water bottle in a position they can reach. Again, in the early days you might have to help them yourself, so be prepared

- Be prepared to pay for an expert to come to your house if you're having trouble. It's worth it if you can afford it, but research and read the reviews first

- Find a support group. There are countless breastfeeding groups that meet in coffee shops in most major towns and cities. OK, so you probably don't need to go yourself, but arrange it for her and drop her off. Lactating mums are a

THE BREASTFEEDING JOURNEY

welcoming bunch and she will get loads of support from joining a group

And last but not least, don't overlook pumping. There may arise an opportunity for you to do some bottle-feeding as well if your partner expresses milk via a breast pump. Many couples choose to do this and it gives dads a chance to feed and bond with their babies. I've spent many a late night or early morning doing this and it was indeed a very satisfying feeling to be involved. So be sure to arm yourself with as much knowledge as you can and get yourself in the thick of things. It's one of the times that your help can make all the difference...guaranteed.

So I'd just like to conclude by saying that despite what you might think, breastfeeding is most certainly not a solo pursuit for women only. Just because you're not doing the actual feeding doesn't mean you can't play a pivotal role. If you and your partner decide to breastfeed then your help and support are critical as to how successful she will be.

Shortcomings

Empty your pockets of righteousness;
add some gasoline and set it on fire.

Once you enter into a committed relationship and decide to have kids, it's important to be aware of your shortcomings as a human being. We all have them and I know I have mine. A lot of people don't take the time to honestly judge themselves, trying to understand how their issues could affect those around them. For example, I'm more than comfortable to say and admit I'm not particularly gifted at anything much. Now that may be a bit of an overstatement but heck, one thing I knew for sure was that I was never going to be good at sports. I had to have special physical education classes as a seven year old because I just couldn't catch a ball. What I lacked in sports I more than made up for in something else; self-awareness. I do excel in self-awareness, almost to an acute level. You don't have to take my word for it. My wife is a psychologist and she says being self-aware is almost a disorder for me.

I'm usually able to understand my actions without any real emotion and I see myself very much in black and white. Being self-aware doesn't mean you're more accustomed to better behaviour though. I'm more able to understand my own behaviour and when I'm to blame for something I rarely shirk responsibility and blame someone else. If I've done wrong, I know I've done wrong and will almost never try to dodge that judgement. The blame game never has a winner, but it does have a lot of losers. When you become parents, you need to set aside the blame game, become more self-aware, and take responsibility for yourself and your actions.

I'm not sure why or when exactly it happened, but for some reason I don't enjoy receiving praise for anything I've done that's been a success. I'm always grateful to receive flattering comments but generally, it makes me feel uncomfortable. I'd rather just be happy in myself knowing that I've done something well. I don't think there is anything particularly wrong with this trait but the unfortunate flip side of this is that I find it a little harder to dish out praise to others. Just ask my younger brother! It's not that I don't want to praise and give out compliments on a job well done, it's just that it doesn't occur naturally to me to do that. I have to remind myself sometimes that it's important for others to have their achievements acknowledged. I'm getting better at this though, and having Lilly-Jo and Huey has made it easier. They help me to recognise that children need lots of praise—and so does your partner. Praise and thanks are important. Mums don't get enough praise or thanks at the best of times, so it's especially important for you to remind them what a terrific job they're doing, particularly if they are the primary caregiver while you're at work all day.

I can also at times be a little unsympathetic when it comes to other people's sicknesses. Maybe it's because I had a bad illness when I was young and I became a bit impervious to feeling awful, so when I finally overcame it I think it had made me a little hardened to being ill. I rarely take time off work even when I am ill now. You could call me a "grin and bear it" kind of guy which can be a bad trait when others are ill. I have to try to always be more understanding when my wife is feeling ill. Having a partner and kids has helped me to become more compassionate. Ever since the kids have come along, I've realised that there is no better feeling than having someone look after you when you're unwell.

Compassion, responsibility, understanding, and praise are all important things to learn and practise. These will help you through the "bad" times when things seem to go off the rails. The thing with parenting, especially in the early days, is that loads of stuff goes wrong. Actually, there are some days when more goes wrong than right, but that's just part of learning. Parenting is something that you learn as you go. Every minute of every day you're probably going to learn something. Inevitably, something goes wrong, but it's really nothing to worry about unless you learn nothing from it. I'm sure I'm not alone in saying that I was pretty stretched both mentally and physically in the early days when Lilly-Jo was little. There were times when I was so tired that my toenails ached. However tired I felt though, I knew Louise was feeling it more. I think that helped me get through those tough moments. Simple things like when Lilly-Jo was teething and no one was sleeping; you haven't lived through "tough" until you come out of the other side of teething! Many times, just surviving into the next minute will be your only goal. Once you stop thinking only about how you feel, and begin to understand your partner's feelings, then somehow things just get easier to cope with. You and your partner are in this together, like castaways clinging to a raft that's being tossed about the ocean.

I admit again that I have my own shortcomings and I hope that sharing them will encourage other dads to be more aware of theirs, and how they might affect their family. Hopefully I've made you think about yourself a little. If, like me, you've got a few colours that are less useful than others, being aware of them makes it easier to avoid circumstances where they come out at entirely inappropriate moments. Trust me, when you've been up for nights on end without proper sleep and downtime, all your true colours will come out. We humans do strange things when we become super tired.

P.S. I also have a very annoying habit of leaving my used towels all over the house, with a particular penchant for placing them on top of fresh-folded laundry. You can guess how well that goes down...Can't you?

Awake Is The New Sleep

At some point every new parent will pay $1000 for 5 minutes sleep.

How much would you pay for an uninterrupted two hours of sleep? At some point during the baby and toddler phase, every parent will sell his or her soul for a good night's sleep; that I can promise you. If you're reading this and think that I have some magical solution to babies and sleep deprivation, then I'm afraid you'll be a bit disappointed. As I constantly say, being prepared for what is about to unfold is always a good start—and that my friends, is what this book is all about. If you know about it, and can prepare for those bits of early stage parenthood that knock many good men to their knees, you'll be ahead of the game. Sometimes the solution is just a good dose of reality.

The first thing you want to consider as a new father is just how tired your partner is going to be. The emotional and physical experience of pregnancy and childbirth, no matter how straightforward, is going to leave them pretty spent. And now, thanks to social media and movie stars, the last few decades have built up huge pressure on mums to get that pre-baby body back and to return to work as soon as possible. You would think that once the birth process was over that your lives would now be filled with joyous fairy tale moments spent cuddling your baby, living life with perfection. Well that's what all forms of the media and social media want you to believe. Don't buy into it! Awake is the new sleep.

As I mentioned before, those first few weeks when you bring home your baby can be full of fear and panic, right alongside happiness and joy. The lack of rest and real sleep can worsen the more negative feelings. It was immensely important to me that Louise enjoy the first few weeks of being a mum as much as she could. Affording her every opportunity to rest along the way was a tiny but huge thing I could do. Before your baby is born, take the time to sit down and think about what you can offer your partner in the early days after the birth. If you have the opportunity to take any kind of paternity leave then please do so. If you have a relative that you both like and trust that can help, then get them involved, even if they just come around every few days and do some laundry for you. You can't even imagine yet how helpful it is to have someone pop in and ask if they can do something as simple as laundry, or a run to the shops for groceries.

Getting back to the lack of sleep issue though, no one, and I mean no one, can fully prepare us dads as to just how tiring parenting can and will be in the early days. I assumed that my vast skill and expertise in late night/early morning partying back in my single days would mean I'd sail through the late nights. Surely I could dust off the cobwebs and trundle off to work the next day. How could a little baby be worse, or even be able to compete with a 14-hour pub crawl? On this account, I was sadly very wrong.

The fatigue and sheer exhaustion of coping with a newborn really is something else. I think all of the unknowns of the experience, only highlights it. As the saying goes, whoever said that "they slept like a baby" probably never had one of their own. For me the hardest part was the broken and constantly interrupted sleep. I'm not good at it. I need a full uninterrupted stretch of sleep to keep me from turning into a cranky beast. It only takes a few days for me to get incredibly irritable. What I am good at though, is early mornings. I am one of those "early to rise" types, and that's one thing that I could use to help with Lilly-Jo. Louise and I worked around that strength, and others, to design a schedule where we shared the load and that helped everyone get some rest.

I can't emphasise how important it is to keep communicating with each other and realise that one tired parent is far better than the two of you being shattered.

So try as much as you can to share the load and pay attention to your partner's state of mind. Knowing when to step in and order her off to bed is vital, but you should be prepared to see that maternal instinct rise up. Maternal instinct, and the need to take 100% care of baby is strong and mums often need a bit of general coaxing to go off for a few hours and rest up. I always liked the times when Louise took a rest and even though they were hard, it's incredible to just sit quietly with your baby lying on you. At this moment, I'm sitting on a couch with a ten day old baby as I write this. It's 5:28 am and I've been here since 4am and I will probably still be here around 7am. Another satisfying thing in this moment is that Louise is resting. I know how tired Louise was today as she had been up all night over the last two nights trying to feed our little one, so she was desperate for some proper rest. There really is no greater gift you can give your lady than the luxurious gift of sleep. It's a win-win because the knock on effect is that she will have more energy to devote to your little one, which will in turn make a happier baby. The trickle-down effect will probably reach you too!

So, dads-to-be, don't be one of those partners who shirks responsibility. In the early days it's very difficult, I'm not going to lie to you. But, it's rewarding to help out and it can really cement the relationship you have with your partner. I dare say she will look back on your efforts and possibly gush to your friends and relatives about just how helpful and understanding you were when things were tough in the early days. Bonus! Don't do it for the acknowledgement though, just do it because it's the right thing to do for your partner and your baby. No one ever became a worse father or partner for being understanding and thoughtful.

#USEDTOBRINGHOMEWINE

What She Wishes You Knew About What It's Like Being A New Mum

When the Mums on my Instagram page speak, you should listen.

amccanse: I wish he understood that when I complain about how much my body changed from carrying babies, that it doesn't mean I regret having them. And that saying, "isn't it worth it'?" doesn't help, because he'll never understand what it's like to give up your body for someone else.

hollyrossi: I want him to know that I loved, and sometimes miss the life we had together for the ten years before we had our children, I also love the life we have now, as crazy and kid-dedicated as it is. I try to set aside time just for him.

What she wishes you knew about what it's like to be a mum

aestherlyienda: I wish he understood that I do not need to ask for help when I obviously do. I want him to understand that the responsibility is for both of us, not just me. Not just because I breastfeed and he doesn't. I hate it when he uses breastfeeding as an excuse for not helping me take care of the baby.

ggbrock: Hormones and sleep deprivation…and the feeling of being stuck at home, inside, for seemingly days on end!!!

kristinnlandry: There is always constant anxiety and thoughts of trying to be the best mom and wife. Balancing all the infant duties, on top of trying not to neglect your marriage or household chores. Then at the end of a long day…

Undressing for a shower and looking at your post-partum body and breastfeeding breasts.

fashionhillz: Like, right now, baby has a sprained ankle and I blame myself. I feel like the worst mom in the whole world. My husband doesn't get it.

kamicar3: It is part of mommy DNA to worry about my baby twenty four hours a day and overly worry about everything.

krakrjak11: Night time routines are extra difficult when I get home, late from work. If he's home before me it would be helpful if he started dinner or a load of laundry…Not wait till I get home to ask "What's for dinner?" when I'm preoccupied about feeding, bathing, playing and putting baby to bed at a decent hour.

ms_harris: Don't look to me for answers on raising our child; I'm learning too. The added pressure of having to direct you in order to receive assistance is both discouraging and crippling. Take an active role in parenting. Read the books/blogs/ask other experienced parents/experiment/whatever it takes. Because that's what I'm doing!

What she wishes you knew about what it's like to be a mum

choresandchatter: The emotional and mental strain of managing little humans all day drains you, and one more person needing you at the end of the day is overwhelming. Especially at the beginning with sleep deprivation.

soyyotu: That I'm not a pro just because a human came out of my body. And just because I am now a stay-at-home-mom, doesn't mean the house is going to be spotless, with homemade dinners and that I'm going to look like a supermodel, once he gets home from work. Being a stay-at-home-mom is so physically and emotionally draining. So I, believe it or not; I AM TIRED.

amags1: I wish he understood I didn't know how much work it would be. I work full time and I try to keep up with everything. Sometimes I just wish I could wake up and he would just say, "Relax, I got this."

sangelica11: I wish he understood my concern for our son when he gets hurt or isn't feeling well. My husband never seems to think anything is a big deal. So he doesn't always agree or understand why I want to take him to the doctor to get checked. Or how I am able to tell the difference between, "I'm not really hurt" cry, versus, "I really hurt myself" cry. He just doesn't trust my instincts.

pregnancyproblems: I wish he realized that it's teamwork. Just because I housed the baby for nine months doesn't mean I have to do all the work when baby arrives too. He works, and I still have school and part time work – and it's a lot to deal with. I feel as though I'm "expected" as the mother, to be the one tending to baby, feeding baby, figuring out which family member is babysitting baby, etc. It's a lot of work for one person and that's why there should be an equal distribution between both of us. I wish, instead of getting frustrated, there was more communication and WANTING to parent.

What she wishes you knew about what it's like to be a mum

jennsayss: Being a new mom is just as scary and if not scarier than being a new dad. You had this beautiful human being in your stomach for nine months and suddenly you feel different about your body, and expected to know how to be a good mom. I feel that moms need that extra praise and assurance that they look good and are doing a good job! It's the little things that matter such as the dad getting up in the night to change the baby so you can feed them. Teamwork is the key!

nmt6813: Whenever my husband would have the baby I would get anxious and say, "Be sure to…" or "Don't forget to…" or "Be careful of…" My head and heart knew that he would not let a single thing happen to our baby, but that motherly instinct just takes over and says… "Protect, protect, protect". It is not the lack of trust or confidence in parenting. Oh, and the hormones! We don't even understand them :)

babyledeverything: I wish he understood that everything doesn't get magically normal once the baby is out of my belly!! I have hormones, those post-pregnancy hormones and inner battles to deal with, like breastfeeding pressure…guilt, and much, much more to deal with. I wish he understood the fourth trimester!

kenziegilly: Short and simple…be nice and helpful, with all baby and home duties.

ingy21: Words of affirmation like "Thank you" and "You're doing great" is much more needed and appreciated more than ever.

cassielj_: I wish he would understand that putting our son to sleep would be so much easier on me if he wouldn't come in during our sleepy time routine and get him all hyped up. Although I love how much fun he is with our son I'd much rather he saved the fun daddy stuff when I need a break, to just be myself for a few minutes.

amynavery: I wish he understood that it is instinct to answer every cry and telling me to "leave him be, he's fine", while in the middle of cleaning or showering or eating, is not helpful! Being around a little more, so I could clean or eat or shower IS in fact helpful.

How To Make A Halo

You can buy all the parts but you still have to put it together yourself.

I was trying to remember the other day what our lives were like before kids came along. Specifically, did we always run out of everything like we do now? I mean we aren't disorganised people but it just seems that no matter what we do there is always some necessity we don't have. As I trudge off to the shops for milk every other night, I try to remind myself that it's not 500 BC and I'm lucky I don't have to chase a cow around the plains in order to milk it.

There is quite a lot you can do as a dad to make sure that the very important baby items are always well-stocked in your house. I wasn't always so great at remembering milk or bread, but I always kept a very watchful eye on all the baby product staples that we used every day. I would even bring them home after work if I thought we needed it. Basically if it helps clean, feed or soothe a baby then you don't want to be running out of it. You will very quickly learn what your own staples are so it's fairly pointless for me to go into too much detail. But items such as diapers, creams (too many to mention) and also, depending on how you are feeding baby, formula

levels, or any breastfeeding-related products should be watched so you know what you have.

The other really important items that we were always running out of were pacifiers (dummies), as they call them in the UK. Stop it. I know what you're thinking and I won't lie! Before Lilly-Jo was born I was also one of those people that swore my child would never use one. You may be swearing it too but I bet you'll find that idea went out the window just like ours did. For us, it took just a few days into our new life with her before we crossed over into "that" crowd. Be prepared! You'll get people telling you that pacifiers do all manner of bad things to your child, like inhibit speech. Honestly, the only thing that inhibits your child's speech is you not talking to them. Anyway I went off on a bit of a tangent there, didn't I...?

My point was that over the last few years we have bought upwards of about fifty of these things and lost roughly forty-seven. I'm convinced that somewhere in our house is a very small creature that scuttles around our floor collecting pacifiers at night and taking them back to his lair for indefinite storage purposes. Maybe inside the missing socks? The most annoying thing about these pacifiers is that Lilly-Jo is fussy with them. She will only consider using the really hard-to-find expensive brands. I tell you, whoever manufactures our little lady's favourites must be laughing all the way to the bank.

My short summary of how you can help keep your house in order wasn't actually short, was it? You'll need to stay on top of this supply and demand. Now isn't the time to be cheap. If it helps, you can always pretend you're hoarding and prepping for the zombie apocalypse. There are plenty of ways to be a Super-Dad and keep that halo shining brightly, and this is just one of them. You don't have to keep a special box full of gear in your house, although the accompanying picture with this chapter is merely an example. A good mental note or scribbled list usually does just as well.

I found over time that a well-kept house means a less-stressed wife. If she is the daytime caregiver of your little one then you should try and execute this chapter as best you can. Happy Wife, Happy Life!

The Bonding Lottery

'Dear Daddy, today I don't like you! Maybe try again tomorrow?' Love, Baby.

I remember saying to Louise when we found out we were having Huey that the law of averages stated clearly we would never get it as easy as we had it with our first baby, Lilly-Jo. While I only said it in jest it actually turned out not to be far from the truth. We couldn't have known how different two babies could be and the comparison between the first three months of their lives was the difference between night and day. Louise will tell you that, with Huey, there is no such thing as night. He basically treats twenty odd hours of the day as, well, the day. While I'll get into the trials and tribulations of that little one later, let's just say if we could bottle his essence and sell it as a drink, we'd be billionaires. There would be late night Clubbing enthusiasts queuing up around the block to get their hands on this all-night party elixir. Humour aside, I wanted to share my bonding experiences with both my babies, as they were so vastly different.

There's been so much written on dads bonding with their new babies that I'm not certain I can offer you anything particularly earth-shattering; nothing of the sort that will truly change your life anyway. I spend a lot of time talking to dads through my business, and if you're feeling a little left out in the cold as a new dad, I can tell you that you're most certainly not alone. Some men express regret they don't, or didn't know the best way to engage a young baby and so they tend to take a backward step. Women can in turn become frustrated at this back-stepping and see it as their partner not wanting to be involved enough. From my observations, some men really, truly do find it hard to bond with a new baby.

Young babies can often spend most of the day glued to mum, so it's difficult sometimes to get a look in. Similarly, I know some dads who actually came into their own as dads when their babies got that little bit older and their responsiveness was more obvious to see. However, if you look broadly at the bonding experience, it follows a different path for both men and women. Sometimes it even differs dramatically from baby to baby. I, personally, never looked at bonding as having some kind of equation or path that must be followed. For me it was simply about being there to do the everyday tasks as much as I could; tasks that ranged from bathing to bottle-feeding and, yes gents, even changing diapers.

Think about this. You are probably more familiar with your baby because you've known about him or her for nine months through mum's belly. Baby hasn't got a clue who you are when he pops out into the world and frankly, he couldn't care at that moment! Think about it, suddenly you are thrust out of the warm, cosy confines of your home into a place where everything is bright, scary, and noisy, so it's not surprising that it takes a bit of time to get used to the surroundings and start feeling the love. The more you are around and are being part of the daily routine, the more you will bond. There is no watershed moment that signifies bonding has occurred but it usually happens with a smile or some serious eye contact. Often, immediately after this moment, baby will start smiling at a plastic bag or used tissue, just to make you feel extra special. I think it's an evolutionary way to keep you on your toes.

Right from the moment she was born, Lilly-Jo and I bonded very quickly. I was very greedy with her and wouldn't let her mum get anywhere near the change table or bath. While she took fairly well to breastfeeding she was also a very enthusiastic bottle feeder, so I spent many early mornings attending to her milk-guzzling while Louise slept. She would also sleep pretty much on anyone so that was nice for our relatives and myself. It's a lovely feeling having a snoring baby cuddle up to you and there were always fights in our house over who would get her. She really enjoyed taking a pacifier, which was a benefit because this can really relax a new baby. As I said earlier, I was dead against them before she came along, but they really suit some babies, and she was one of them.

Huey had a different way of doing things when he arrived a few years later. The poor little guy was born with chronic colic and spent the first few months of life in what seemed to be a great deal of discomfort. It's so hard as a parent when they can't tell you what is wrong with them. We tried everything to soothe him and nothing seemed to work. The only way he seemed to settle was by being breastfed, and we believed his "comfort feeding" was able to soothe his tummy. Unfortunately, he would then spend the whole night crying in pain. It was a vicious, sad circle. The first few months were pretty hard on all of us. I never had many opportunities in those first few months to bond with him. He would scream if I picked him up and more often than not, he wouldn't take a bottle, so I couldn't snuggle-feed him either.

It sounds awful to say, but there were moments when I wished that time would speed up, partly so he wouldn't be in pain anymore but also so I could have him to myself a bit more; and of course so he wouldn't scream bloody murder at me. Even at six months old, I still haven't taken him anywhere alone yet. As Grandma says, he's like a ticking time bomb, and when he goes off, you're going to need mummy there pretty darn quick. In the last few weeks we have started to see little glimpses of his actual personality as his body starts to heal from his colic. He is really a very smiley baby with a truly goofy personality underneath all that crying. He's so different from his sister who was the most serious, suspicious baby you'd ever meet. We hardly got a single smile from that one in the early days. Knowing her now, I am sure that she was just far too busy for silliness as she was trying to calculate how best to control the entire household and all the adults in it.

So take it from me, nothing is guaranteed in the world of babies when it comes to bonding and being a daddy. After experiencing both extremes the best advice I can give you is to take each day as it comes, and don't give up even when you think all hope is lost. It will come around, but nothing worthwhile ever comes easy. Every day I still look for the light at the end of the tunnel, but the difference now, as compared to a few months ago, is that I don't mind how long I'm in the tunnel anymore so long as I'm heading in the right direction.

How Soon After The Birth Can I Play Golf?

*Excuse me sir, can you tell me again
how long a piece of string is?*

This isn't really a chapter about how soon you can return to either the golf course or your chosen activity after the birth of your baby. It's more about how long things will take to return to normal. I'm not sure I should be using the term "normal" here, as things will never really go back to the old ways and routines that you knew. Your lives are forever changed once a new baby comes. You need to understand that someone (someone being the baby) will move the goal posts in your game of "normal" that you had been quite happily playing with your wife or partner. It's OK though, don't worry too much. You'll get used to it. It just takes a little time. While I don't consider myself much of a golfer, I have been a very committed surfer since I was about fourteen. I grew up in Australia so surfing was a big part of my life. I don't suppose living in London has ever really been the ideal location to continue that pursuit but I make it

work even if it does involve ridiculous amounts of travel for very little reward. I can remember feeling a little apprehensive about how, and if, my love affair with the ocean would continue after the birth of our first baby. Let me rephrase that; I was quite worried that I'd never again find time to make that half day drive I needed to get me from London to the coast and back.

It's very important to me to get out and surf. I guess in a way it provides my self- esteem with the constant propping up it needs and helps me clear my mind and recharge. All men like to think they are good at something on an individual level and I'm no different. A good few hours bobbing up and down and hacking into waves always makes me feel like a better person. It used to be that I did it partially to impress girls (don't we all do something to impress girls?) but now I just do it solely for myself. Granted, in reality my agility hasn't quite kept up with my mind's idea of what my physical self can actually do.

I can still remember vividly my last surfing trip before Lilly-Jo was born. Louise and I had agreed that I'd be no further than one hour away from home, five weeks before the birth. Given that I knew I wouldn't be going anywhere for at least two months after the birth I really wanted to make the most of it. What better way to close out another chapter of "childless" than to head out surfing with my best friend since I was four. We had a shabbily arranged tent closer to a pub than a beach; and there was lots of laughing and snoring. It was a totally beaut weekend—as they say in Australia, and seeing as I was convinced I'd never ride a wave again, it was certainly a very nice way to go out.

That fear that I would never surf or have time of my own has, of course, turned out to be totally unjustified. Thankfully, and over the months following the birth, we saw our new family routine gradually start to take shape and return to some kind of normality.

I think for me there was no rush really to get back on the horse, as they say. I could never have left Louise to go off and do my own thing without knowing she was either fine by herself or had someone around to help. Please remember that while you might be desperate to get back to whatever it is you enjoy outside of family life, don't forget that your partner might be desperate to do the same too. Women don't stop having interests just because they have kids, and you should definitely make this your mindset. It's important for both parents to continue to pursue interests and adventures outside of the family circle; just don't get carried away.

One of the great things about my partnership with Louise is that I never really had to discuss my desire to get back to the beach. I didn't have to. She already knew I would want to and she was OK with that. What I did to help was to give her as much support and time outside the house as she needed. In the early days when she was stuck in a chair at home for hours a day feeding Lilly-Jo while I was at work, time for her was important. Give and take—remember that and you won't go wrong.

By doing that regularly you instantly make it easier for yourself when you want a bit of alone-time. Partners who want the best for each other realise very early on that the door swings both ways... make sure you know it too.

Ships In The Night

You'll hit the odd iceberg...
but you don't have to end up like Leo.

There are downsides to having children. I just wanted to say that straight away to get it out in the open. To be bluntly honest, having children turns your life upside down in a split second. There is no other way to put it. What once was, will never really be again and you can either keep trying to be the version of you that you were, or you can adapt and become the person you need to be. Sometimes the negatives are the things we avoid talking about for fear of upsetting our partner or being judged by other parents. It is very important that we do talk about these things, so we don't sit and stew.

I wanted to use this chapter to talk about some of the issues that can affect new parents. Some of them affected us, and some didn't, but they can happen to anyone. I've seen enough marriages suffer from strain during the early years of family life to know that the relationship you have with your partner needs to be a top priority, no matter what else is going on in your lives. I'm going to totally throw myself to the wolves by freely admitting that I'm included

14 - 12 - 2015

10:23 pm zZ^Z (finally)

in the 99% of men out there who have issues expressing their emotions. I maintain that there was no reason that my upbringing caused this, it's more than likely a product of our species.

Apparently, as Google tells me, this lack of expression is caused by a part of your brain (or lack of) called Corpus Callosum. He's the guilty one, Your Honour! He's the one who kidnapped my feelings! No, but seriously, it's a neurological issue, and without wanting to get too scientific, it goes a bit like this: Both males and females have this particular part of the brain that works to connect the left and the right hemispheres. In the fairer sex, it's much bigger and that ultimately allows them to THINK and FEEL at the same time. Imagine! I just can't even fathom that because I can't even eat a sandwich and think at the same time. This probably explains why you should never attempt to argue with your partner as they are able to call on combined senses instead of your pitiful solo one. I think it's worth starting with that very basic lesson in the anatomy of the human brain as it gives you a better idea of how men and women differ, and how, every now and then, they experience difficulties in their relationships.

One of the biggest problems with adjusting to life with your new family is the lack of time you will get to spend together as a couple. It does get better as your child grows, and your routines with them become more settled, but in the early days it's very difficult to do anything other than live in the now. As a direct result of this lack of real time you spend together, you can often see a gradual breakdown in communication. I don't mean the absence of deep and meaningful conversations, but just the bare-bones of the interactions that you probably took for granted before. You may find that because you're both so focused on the new baby, you forget to ask about how the day went or even forget to ask about the wellbeing of your partner. It may also be that you are not picking up on the usual things you would normally pick up on, like when your other half isn't as well in herself as she should be.

The good news about this is that you'll be so busy early on, especially in the first six months, that you probably won't notice the absence of that time together. I think there is a certain period in the early days that you just have to write off when it comes to quality time with your partner. I never worried about it too much, and as long as you're helping as much as you can to get life settled, I don't think there is much else you can do. I do urge you to make the time to connect or at least pay attention to the non-verbal things that your partner does. This is very important!

While we luckily had no experience with post-natal depression, personally, I knew enough about it to pay attention to the signs, just in case. With this illness there are often a variety of symptoms, from general unhappiness to feelings of sadness and guilt and these can often be red flags. If you even suspect for a second that your partner is experiencing any of these, you should find help for her immediately. Certainly don't just advise her that she should see her doctor; you need to physically take her to seek help. Being aware of, and watching out for problems like post-natal depression, is just one of the reasons it's important that you keep the lines of communication open. As I've said time and again, if you aren't even aware that something might be an issue then you've probably already lost the battle against it. Be vigilant.

It's going to be hard for you to become a better communicator and to show your feelings, but it's essential for the general health of your relationship. It's a fact not lost on me because I struggle with it personally, and have always done so. The problem is that you can't get away with it as much when children come along, because they simply change the dynamic of your relationship. You need to keep up with those changes. While I don't want to scare you, it's inevitable that you will at times become *ships in the night*. During the early period of raising your little ones, you may just pass each other in the hallway during shift changes with your baby. Often with us, no words were exchanged, but a simple hug was enough to remind us we were in it together. Sometimes it's the very simple things you can do as a new dad to keep the ship steady. No one is expecting you to go all Dr Phil and express every single emotion you feel, because that just wouldn't be right, but you can surely try and open up just a bit more...It will make things easier.

The Flat Pack Dimension

My goal in life is to find that Swedish guy and punch him on the nose!

The realm of flat pack furniture is a bit like the excruciating pain of being struck by lightning; if you don't know it's coming then at least it's a surprise, right? And everyone likes surprises, don't they? I want to tell you it's going to be OK. I want you not to feel the fear I've felt...but I can't. If you're reading this and haven't really ever had to spend quality time in a room with odd shaped bits of painted timber, and weird nuts and bolts, then it's probably better you stop reading now.

For research purposes I've learned that some Swedish bloke who was trying to fit a table into his car invented flat pack furniture. He came up with this horrendous idea because (a) he was clever and (b) he obviously had no empathy or sympathy or love for his fellow man. He then went on to market the idea and helped turn flat packing into the billion-dollar business it is today.

The thing about flat pack furniture is that it should be good—but really, it's not. It's cleverly disguised in those glitzy catalogues as so easy-peasy that no one ever thinks how difficult, or time-consuming it's truly going to be to put together. Actually, that's not true for me. I always think about how long it's going to take to put something together, when I see a pile of boxes in our lounge room, and Louise with a beaming smile handing me a screw driver. The size of her smile is often directly proportional to the time, energy and cursing that goes into a project.

It used to be (or so I'm told) that all your nursery equipment arrived off the back of a truck, fully assembled, and with several large burly men who would jostle it up the stairs and place it wherever you wanted it to go. But now in the modern age, rather than let someone else do the dirty work, we parents are up trying to make sense of those crazy line drawings at 1am, and a seemingly inexhaustible amount of nut and bolt hardware. I can't tell you how many times I have been there, on the floor with glazed eyes, with drawings and hardware surrounding me! Cribs, cupboards, nursing chairs, a storage unit...I've done it all and made every single mistake possible. These blunders range from not following the instructions properly (don't wag your finger at me, you of the female persuasion) and putting everything together back-to front, to closely following the instructions, and still putting everything together back to-front.

I've also been foiled many a time by mixing up all the various hardware components, which in my own defence can be very similar in size, but will not work in one hole or the other. Then there was the time I ripped a packet of screws apart with a little bit too much gusto and then spent a few lovely hours on my hands and knees trying to find the tiny components in thick carpet. Of course it's thick carpet, you don't think it would be short-pile carpet to make it easy now, do you?

I believe it was shortly after this incident that I joined a Facebook group called *Men against Flat Pack*. It has a few thousand members but they are always looking for new recruits eager to share their tales of woe. Seeing how it's more than likely you'll be involved in this travesty of construction soon though, I thought I'd share a few of my survival tips:

1. Always, always have alcohol readily available, and if required, chilling in the fridge. You'll need it by the time you hit page 2 of the instruction manual.

2. Never, ever think you don't need to follow the instructions, even for the simplest items. I've been in construction and engineering for twenty years and I learned my lesson on this the hard way.

3. Whatever you pick up, put it back down in exactly the same place. Mixing and matching hardware is neither advised nor encouraged. However, this mistake can be managed by following step one.

4. Whenever you finish an item make sure you keep the instructions and the special assembly tools that came with it. Your partner may gift the item to a friend when the baby grows out of it and you'll suddenly realise you can't take the thing apart without those tools if it's too big to fit in a car.

5. Inevitably, you will spend hours putting something together and right at the end realise that one shelf, or likewise, is upside down and thwarts any chance of your being able to finish it correctly and promptly. If this occurs, please go back to step one.

6. Once you've been around the block a few times as I have, you'll come to realise that flat pack furniture is a bit like a game of snakes and ladders. No one can ever truly master it. Well, except for those people who do it for a living and can be easily found on Google for bargain basement prices!

Actually, maybe I should have made that step one...

The Money Bonfire

Babies are the stealthiest pickpockets you'll ever meet.

There is no way that you can escape, prepare for, or even save for it; raising children is bizarrely expensive. I actually have a few cheapskate friends and I can't wait until they have children, just so they can finally loosen up and stop being such annoying penny-pinchers. Don't get me wrong, there is nothing bad about being frugal at times—but there's a time and a place for it. For example, the time for frugality isn't when your child needs diapers and you have to pay full price at the corner store because there's no wholesale outlets open at 2am; you just can't drag your heels about spending the cash.

It's a lot easier to be cautious and thrifty with money when you're single. There is time to shop around and compare prices and gaze for hours at the computer screen trying to find the best deals and bargains. When you are single, there's plenty of time to kill in the supermarket milling around the aisles, trying to find the best price on those imported olives you've been thinking about eating all week. You'll soon come to realise that a lot of the things you used to buy, pre-baby, were things you wanted, but not actually needed. The arrival of a baby into this mix not only throws a spanner in the works, but practicality stops the whole machine functioning in its usual capacity. You simply won't have the time or the energy to be leisurely with your spending because you'll be entering a dark abyss also known as "the world of baby gear". This is why it's important to focus and spend your time and energy wisely a few months before the due date to make sure you nail down the baby basics. Remember that your partner will grow ever more tired as the due date looms, so don't leave it too late! Your partner won't be thrilled marching around showrooms at eight months pregnant looking for things you've promised to buy but have been procrastinating about buying.

Speaking of procrastination, this might actually be the best time to mention decorating the nursery. Two things are critical to the success of your relationship when it comes time to planning your new baby's room and they are:

1. Listen to your wife's decorating ideas and **execute them correctly**,
2. Listen to your wife's decorating ideas and execute them **well before the baby arrives**.

Many men have chosen not to heed this advice and have lived to regret their complacency. You've all heard about nesting, right? Nesting is basically when your partner becomes obsessive about the state of the new baby's room (and the kitchen and the closets and the laundry and—and—and). It's really important that everything is as she wishes, right down to the correct shade of lilac and the matching bedding. Right. Now there's a short intermission into the world of nurseries...Now back to the task at hand. The thing with baby products, or what I've found at least, is that the really good ones cost a little more money. As I said, there is a time and place for being frugal but no baby of ours was ever going to have a feeding bottle, or other basic necessity, of suspect quality. It just isn't worth the worry! If you're wondering what feeding bottle I'm talking about, think "cheap plastics" leeching chemicals; or budget diapers that leak in the middle of the night. Wait! Did I mention cheap diapers that leak and wake baby at 2am? (E.g. you wake at 2am). Yes? Don't do that to yourself. As I mentioned earlier, I think it's important to nail down your basic purchases fairly early on in the pregnancy to avoid a chaotic third trimester. There are countless essential baby item lists out there on Google so it's fairly easy to work out what your basic needs are. As long as you've got yourself the following:

1. a car seat
2. stroller
3. baby clothes
4. diapers
5. feeding equipment, and
6. somewhere for the baby to sleep,

You're fairly good to go. I have yet to meet a mum-to-be who didn't have all of this covered, so really all we dads need to do is become the enabler for them to get it. If you are stuck on brands, and choosing the right equipment, I would recommend checking out BabyGuyNYC. While I generally don't hand out endorsements, he has a terrific website and Facebook page with cutting edge reviews. Basically, from what I can tell, he travels the world talking about baby gear, while surviving on a diet of margaritas and oversized cookies. Trustworthy? Yes I believe so. Well worth a look if you do get stuck.

It is inevitable, however, that you will buy things that you don't actually need and there isn't really much you can do to stop that happening. Sometimes babies grow so fast that they never actually get to wear all of their outfits. This is why it's a good idea not to buy clothes too far in advance. Be aware also, that just because another parent recommends something to you, it may not work for your requirements. This is the time when you might have to police certain purchases when it comes to baby gear. I have been to enough baby expos to know just how huge the baby product industry is. There is literally something for everything - and even something for the everything that has yet to be thought about! It's hard not to be drawn in to the craziness.

Nail down the basics first before you buy the white-noise emitting teddy bear that doubles as an espresso machine! Also note that it's worth considering buying items that are gender neutral. I'm mainly referring to colours here, but if your second baby is a boy, as mine was, then it's nice to not have everything in twelve shades of pink.

While I'm talking numbers, let's talk about relatives. As mentioned in the chapter on visitors, you'll be inundated with them in the early days. These grandparent-type folk are generally at a stage in life when there is a little spare cash floating around. As a parent, it is a joyous moment when these folk dust off their wallets and purses and offer to cough up for essential baby items. If this happens, it's certainly not the time to be shy! Put in your requests for goods or better still, just ask for blank cheques!

That's even easier. If the money isn't flowing as desired, then just resort to guilt trips about the fact that their only grandchild will not have the right equipment for his or her development or safety! That should seal it for you. I'm half-joking here and you should keep the cash flow of your pensioner parents in mind. For many grandparents, sacrificing a round of golf or an extra day in the country so that the grandbaby will have a new stroller is worth it!

Regardless of what ideas you have on spending money, try to remember your partner's feelings. She is in fact growing you a small human, and she will be ever so excited about little things that might not seem so important to you. Socks were Louise's obsession. She loved to buy bucket loads of them and then bring them home to stare at while she talked about the little feet that were going to go in them soon. I tell you, it was worth the expense to see her so happy!

Life and budgets can get crazy at times with a new baby on the way, but try to go along with it. It doesn't hurt to keep a close eye on your budget as you remember that you'll be shelling out money for a good twenty-plus years to come.

Need help?
babyguygearguide.com

For Every First There Will Be A Last

*Savouring the last days of
that little hand clasping yours.*

There are so many exciting moments in the first few years of your child's life that it's pretty hard to comprehend them all at once. My most favourite "first" moment of Lilly-Jo was the evening she laughed for the first time; I mean she truly laughed and didn't just make a sound that might have been a laugh. We were drying her off on the dining room table from her bath and I was dropping cotton balls on her nose just because that's something that I started doing, in the hopes it would make her laugh and smile. She was looking a bit bemused as they softly landed on her face but then all of a sudden, she let out the most enormous cackle! It's one of the most infectious things I had ever heard. Trust me, when a baby laughs you laugh too.

Then there is the first time they walk, which is right up there with the moon landing! Louise and I actually couldn't wait for

Lilly-Jo to get to bed that first night, so we could message every-one we knew and show them the video. If I remember, Louise even started messaging people she didn't know to tell them the good news. Now most of you won't have been lucky enough to see your own first steps on film but every kid born post-iPhone 3, is going to have many of their "firsts" recorded for posterity. Think about that for a second and pause to remember what a wonderful thing technology can be. My parents, who live in Australia, never miss a moment of their granddaughter growing up, because of technol-ogy. I actually believe the magic of WhatsApp has allowed them to "know" her and to feel closer to her when they come to visit.

So, what did I mean when I said, "For every first, there will be a last"? One day when you take your child out, they won't need to hold your hand or won't need help getting up the stairs. One day, they won't need your help for many things. Even now at the age of three, Lilly-Jo is fighting for independence every time we go out. I know the days of that little hand being glued to mine are num-bered. I also know that bedtime stories will one day come to an end and that's very sad as it's been a very big part of my life for what seems like forever.

Things that your kids grow through happen so gradually that when they are over, it seemed like a blink and a flash. Life itself is much the same—but with children, it's magnified so much more. One thing I know for sure is that I will miss coming home and open-ing the door to hear the sound of little feet running towards me. One day, she will stop running to me and I will no longer hear tiny footsteps as I turn the key. Although I know it's coming, I can't even bear to think about not getting a hug every time I come home from work. By the time I was seven or eight, I'd stopped running to meet my parents at the door and although I've never asked them, I won-der if they remember the first day I didn't come bounding towards them.

How did it feel when that day came? Were they sad? Were they happy to see their child had changed from a little person who needed them every second, into a confident child who was secure in their place in life? It must have twanged the heart to realise that their little one didn't need to greet them like a long lost friend, even when they just went out to the shops for thirty minutes. I just hope that every dad who reads this chapter realises how important it is to appreciate those moments; these moments won't always last.

The main reason I wrote this chapter is because soon enough Lilly-Jo will be starting school, and I imagine, sadly, that then she might rather spend Sunday (which was always our special day) with her friends rather than with me. This explains why, for the last few months, I've been putting in an extra special effort to make those 'Daddy Sundays' as fun and exciting as I can. There is no point in my telling you to appreciate something unless I'm doing it myself; believe me I am!

So play with your young kids, like it's your last day on earth! Even though you know it won't be the last time you get them all to yourself, treat it like it is. I imagine that in the future, when they are grown up, Louise and I will pine for the time when they needed us more or hugged us more. Don't be complacent, whatever you do! They are only small for such a short period of time and it's a time that you will never be able to get back. Trust me, you will miss it.

Hide And Seek

Wait until they make you "hide" together.

If there is one thing I can promise you about fatherhood, it's this; at no point in your child's later life will you be able to use money to buy time. You will never, ever be able to buy back the time you didn't spend with your children.

Make time to play with your kids. Don't think about, or say, 'I should' take the time; just do it. Making time to play with your child, especially in the very early years as a father, is pretty much the greatest gift you can give. At the time I wrote this Lilly-Jo was just turning three and like every other kid, she was crazy for play-time. It wasn't always easy to take time out to play with her. I'd get home maybe only an hour before her bedtime and it can some-times be difficult, especially after a long commute, to walk in the door ready to be the "shopkeeper" or the "customer" in her [crazy] game of shops. What I found during these first few years was that the theme of playtime changed almost every week and I learned how it was really important to let her dictate the nature of the play. Allowing yourself to be led by your child's imagination and becom-ing a part of the make-believe, bonds you in the moment. Just going along with her ideas shows her that you're one hundred percent enjoying the "play".

So remember, let your child dictate the nature of the play. It will make things easier and you will actually enjoy being a part of the ever-changing and ongoing development of your child. Playtime is an important part of childhood development, and yes, adult development too.

One of the first and fondest memories I have of Lilly-Jo playing a "game" was shortly after she learned to walk, and also to clap her hands. Her favourite thing to do at that time was to stumble out of the room and then run back in clapping. She would then expect everyone else to start clapping with her, which of course we did. Looking back, I see how much she enjoyed the control she had over us.

If we were to skip forward a few months, you would find me involved in a seemingly endless game of hide and seek with her, as that was her favourite game. Trust me though, you haven't lived until you've played hide and seek with a toddler. Don't ever skip an invitation to play, no matter what game it is! Most of the time I had to "hide" her first and then "find" her; you're following, right? Nothing in the world of toddler hide and seek, in my experience, makes any sense at all. Although, strangely the kids believe it makes perfect sense. As far as hide and seek goes, just wait until your child makes you both 'hide" together. It was exactly during one of these crazy playtime moments, when I was standing in a dark closet with Lilly-Jo that we were actually hiding in the same place; right next to each other. In the midst of this game came one of those defining moments of fatherhood where I actually understood a part of the mystery. I realised how important it was that I was there with her, hiding in the closet, doing exactly what she wanted. I also understood, in that moment, that being good at playtime as an adult is all about forgetting you are one.

I have to admit that playing "Shops" was my favourite playtime adventure. Moving on to playing this newest game every night after work was a satisfying time for me. When we played, we would gather arbitrary amounts of random stuff from the house and lay it all out on the bed. A cash register I had bought for her birthday was also on the bed. We would take turns being the shopkeeper.

While none of it made sense at the time, I managed to teach her a bit about counting. Even though almost everything in her shop was either free or cost "2 twenty dollars" (in her words) she still learned about counting. Playtime brings out more than just a creative side. It also is a chance to learn without being taught, and without knowing that we are learning. It's invaluable to all of us, at any age. At the time of writing this, I'm still playing this with her. I enjoy these games and these times because I know it's all going to end pretty soon, and that makes me incredibly sad.

Playtime with your child is such a fleeting moment, and it changes daily. Make sure you're a part of it as much and as often as you can be. Be sure that when you are in the moment of playtime that you are really there and checked-in. Although when they grow up they might not really remember each and every one of these play sessions, they do live for them. They love these play moments in the present and that is where they are happiest.

Don't worry that all of your hours of play will be forgotten because in the end, they will not be. Most of the happiest friends I have known, including myself, look back on their childhood and remember mum and dad being there, every day, for fun more than anything else. We don't fondly remember the chores or the work that our parents have done but the times they have spent with us. Think about it for a moment yourself.

And one day your children may be at a dinner, or sitting in a bar with a close friend or partner describing a lovely, fun childhood. Even though you might not be there to hear it, you'll have seen the results of your endeavours.

Life Advice, Part 1

Dear Lilly-Jo,

Life is short, *munchkin*...

One day you'll wake up and there won't be time to do the things you'll always want to. Make sure you live your dreams. If you're ever lost and confused don't forget to ask your dad! I spent years doing things I didn't really like, so I'm well qualified to point you in the right direction.

Your mum and I put in an extraordinary amount of work to make sure you had the best possible upbringing. Your mum was especially tireless in this regard.

We don't mind what you do with your life but make sure you do it right. You'll know you are if you can still roll out of bed with a hangover and look forward to the day ahead, and your place in it.

Try not to worry too much about boys. Honestly we are a dime a dozen for smart and pretty things such as yourself. I tried to impress your mum with psychology nonsense when I first met her! Thankfully she saw through that rubbish and I'm sure you will too when the time comes. Just make sure you don't ever call or text a boy first! I don't care how much you like them. It doesn't work that way with us as we are here to impress you, not the other way round.

If you're in doubt, give them my number and I'll happily have a chat to them!

Don't waste your time with idiots, and don't bother giving second chances to people who try to drag you down. There are so many cool people in the world desperate to meet you! I know this, as I was one of them in a delivery room back in 2012. Oh, and don't forget you're half Australian BTW! But forget about their beer. It's rubbish! Take your own when you go and visit Nanny and Grandpa.

Good luck.

Lots of love from your Dad

NB: While I am fully aware that Australia produces some amazing beer, my memories (or lack thereof) tend to centre around those God-awful Hahn Ice 30 blocks of the 90s. I do apologise; I had no money and that's all I could afford.

What Dads See, What Mums see

*The road is actually a moat
and full of hungry alligators.*

While I've always tried very hard to be a supportive and understanding husband, there are plenty of times when I've failed miserably. You probably will too, and maybe you'll know it, or maybe you won't, but I hope you know because knowing helps, a lot.

A really good example of a big fail on my part was the very first time my wife and I took Lilly-Jo out in her stroller, when she was just a few days old. Most parents probably recall the first public outing with their newborn as a fairly harrowing and nerve-wracking stint; and we were no different. In the first weeks after the baby arrives, your house becomes somewhat of a sanctuary where you can control the environment to a certain extent. It took us both a couple of days to get confident enough to take our baby out into that uncontrollable abyss that is our very safe, friendly neighbourhood. Don't get me wrong, my neighbourhood is great, as I said. I say "abyss" because each new thing that you do with your baby brings odd feelings of fear. Don't laugh, even the act of pushing a stroller on a sunny day in a controlled environment like your own

neighbourhood can feel as if you're walking on a tightrope with snapping alligators waiting below.

So, getting back to our first outing. There we were, very cautiously walking along the street towards our local park. Louise was noticeably nervous and I knew she was keeping watch for escaped convicts who were lurking out there, waiting to kidnap us. Me, I was just constantly eyeing the sky looking for any rogue pterodactyls that might swoop down and pluck our little bundle from her stroller. Now I don't know if it was a combination of nerves or the fact that I hadn't slept for days, but when I arrived at the edge of the road across from the park I looked both ways and started across. Suddenly I felt a force grab my arm and pull both the stroller and myself a good three feet back onto the footpath. Given that the stroller and I combined must have weighed well over 200lbs, I turned, expecting to see the Incredible Hulk. To my surprise, the Incredible Hulk was none other than my wife, and a very unimpressed wife at that!

What followed was a pretty public telling off, and rightly so I'd say. It was the very first road we had crossed with our baby and I had neither consulted, nor waited for Louise. Although we laugh about it now, it was serious and it made me realise very quickly that there is perhaps a different thought process for men and women when it comes to fear, especially with a newborn. I had, I guess, engaged the safety aspect of crossing that road in my head so I alone had deemed it safe to cross. However, Louise (possibly) had expected a little consultation on the matter. It was definitely a moment that I will never forget and gave me a little insight into the inner workings of a new mum's mind. Of course, I would never do anything that is really unsafe with Lilly-Jo, but, as her dad, I have involved her in quite a lot of rough and tumble stuff. I think that's just what dads are programmed to do. I do try to be understanding about my wife's concerns but it's hard for me not to encourage Lilly-Jo to climb high or take on the biggest slide at the playground. Mind you, I'm there to catch her every time when she needs catching but once she has mastered something, I generally stand back, let her explore and give her encouragement.

Luckily, Lilly-Jo absolutely loves going out with me on our adventures—partly because she knows I'll let her push the boundaries a little bit more than her mum. It's just another one of those things that most dads do that drive mums crazy. There could be worse things.

It's been a steep learning curve, and I'm still learning that I need to make sure I take my wife's feelings into account when it comes to our kids. It's important to remember that your wife has carried your baby for nine months and that means she has concerns about accidents happening that may be a bit more extreme than yours. Dare I say these concerns are sometimes truly and unnecessarily crazy? I must remember to heed my own advice, right? Keep this all in mind before you career into situations head-on with your little ones. At the very least, be accepting of your wife telling you off, if and when something happens.

Be The Dad You Want To Be, Not The One On TV

TV is highly edited, life is not.

It's hard in this day and age to be the parent you want to be, and not feel intimidated by all the imagery that's blasted out to us on television and social media platforms, like Facebook and Instagram. Perfect parents are everywhere and they're posting or blogging themselves into our lives in an endless supply of perfectly manicured images. Long gone are the days when only famous people were famous. Today, all you need is a family and a smart phone and you too can create your own bit of celebrity.

I marvel at how different things are now compared to what it must have been like when my parents were raising me. We are connected to everyone we know through social media, but at the same time, it seems like we are totally disconnected. We can see every detail of our friends' lives plastered all over our phones on a daily basis. This gives us insights into the family lives of other people that would have seemed like an invasion of privacy even as little

as fifteen years ago. Every day we are seeing the very best snippets of other people's lives and yes, we are uploading the best moments of ours. In reality we are probably only seeing a fraction of what really goes on. I'm sure that what ends up on the cutting room floor would paint a very different reality of what really goes on behind closed doors.

Although I can't really speak for other parents, I have suffered from bouts of inadequacy at times when confronted with some of the things I see on social media. There's the single dads raising daughters, who went to hairdressing schools just so they could learn to make their little girls' hair as good as the other mums did. Or those handymen who make the most amazing bunk beds for their kids, complete with slides that look like rocket ships, or racing cars. I'm not trying to say these things aren't amazing. They are amazing. It's just that it always makes me feel like I'm not good enough. I can't do things like that for my kids due to the time I have to spend at work.

While I do the best I can every day, I just don't understand where people find the time to do and create all these amazing experiences that I see and read about all the time. I mean, for me, making sure I don't burn lunch on Sunday, and keeping the kids safe from hepatitis, is probably about as successful a day as I can hope for. I can't imagine that I am alone in this regard, and I'm sure other parents share similar feelings to mine.

The picture perfect lives and craft projects on social media are an illusion of sorts. What we see on people's personal pages is likely not a true portrayal of what actually happens in reality. Instagram, in particular, is a world of pretty white images portraying the kind of family life you might expect to find in a parallel universe of daisies, rainbows and leprechauns. I often marvel at the way some parents are able to get their little ones to pose so dutifully and flawlessly in front of the camera, without a pixel out of place. The cynical part of me is quietly smiling; knowing how much bribery (chocolate buttons) it probably took to get them there in the first place. That's not to say I'm against these types of social media displays nor am I saying that you shouldn't enjoy following pages like this. Of course you should!

However, I think it's really important to take it all with a pinch of salt. The people who own these accounts are likely experiencing tantrums and all manner of other rambunctious behaviours. The bits you see are the golden rays of family life that appear randomly throughout anyone's day.

This chapter is very applicable to mums as well, considering how much pressure they're under sometimes to be perfect. A really good example of this is the pressure to return to pre-baby weight after the birth. Nothing can fill a tired new mum with rage more than a celebrity mum back in her skinny jeans, two weeks post-partum. What you don't realise is that they probably have a personal chef, a trainer and more than likely a nanny or two. It's super important to be understanding as a partner and know that while they will always be a little sensitive about certain things, nothing is more important than their health and happiness. You should reinforce that as often as you are able to.

Even though I mentioned at times being affected by social media, I generally maintain a positive state of mind. Although I do marvel at the super dads out there in the virtual world, I know what my strengths are as a dad and I'm proud of them. While I am writing a book on fatherhood, I hope it's taken in the open and honest way I've intended it. Maybe I can't do a double plaited ponytail, or afford to take my kids on five star holidays to the Caribbean, but I can play a bloody good game of hide and seek.

So do your best to be the best dad you can be, and while it's only human nature to be a little envious of others, use it as motivation to improve your own qualities. My only real goal with my kids is to raise very balanced humans who see the worth in themselves, and see the world for exactly what it is, both good and bad. You can't really capture that in an Instagram picture, but you'll see that image everyday yourself as they grow to be the best people they possibly can be.

Breadwinning

Bringing home the bacon, and cooking it too!

Finding the balance between work and home life has been one of the biggest challenges I've faced as a parent. Unless you were clever enough to buy Apple shares thirty years ago, you're probably much like myself, and you struggle to pay the bills every month. The big downside is that paying the bills has you chasing time and trying not to miss too much of your kids' childhood while you are stuck at the office until all hours of the night and day. I have a bit of a love/hate relationship with my job—but probably for different reasons than you might think.

Back in the days when I was single I couldn't really have had it better in terms of my job. I have been a welder since I was eighteen, and, as far as trades go, it's not a bad one to have. When I moved to London I discovered that the policies of past governments meant that apprenticeships were all but non-existent. Unfortunately this lack of apprenticeships had been the norm for twenty years. What that meant was that people in my line of work were very much in demand. The pay rates weren't amazing and you had to work 70+ hours a week, but with no dependents and cheap living, I was able to travel the world for years. I only returned to London to do contract work when I needed to fund my next adventure. There aren't that many jobs out there which offered this freedom, and I loved the

lifestyle it afforded me at the time. Although it was a great experience while it lasted, in the end I was tired of living out of a suitcase, and by the time I met Louise, I was ready for a more settled life.

The negative thing about being a welder in the UK and having a family, is that to earn a more-than-decent wage, you have to work a lot of overtime. The struggle that I've had since having kids is trying to find the balance between work and home time. I know I'm not alone and all the other dads at my work are much the same. It simply isn't possible for me to pay the bills without working six days a week.

Working this many days during the week really only leaves me two hours or so in the evening and Sundays to spend with the kids. However, there is an upside to this work schedule. Believe it or not, it's led me into a very positive frame of mind in that the time I do spend with them is real quality time. My kids enjoy it very much as well, but you can read all about that in another chapter. I don't want to make it seem like I'm being ungrateful. I understand I'm lucky to even have a good job when so many people around the world have so little work. I'm not going to spend this chapter apologising for that, so you can all put the violins away—for now, at least.

I had hoped, for as long as I can remember, that one day I'd start a business of my own. It was never a case of my not having an idea that was viable, but more a question of motivation. Although to be fair, I have had my share of mad ideas. The crazy thing is that it wasn't until I had a family that I finally decided that it was time to roll my dice into the world of business. I know! It's a crazy time right? It all started around the time we were starting to wean Lilly-Jo from milk to solid food. Being that I do pretty much all the cooking in our house, I decided that I would take sole charge of all the cooking and pureeing of her tiny first tastes in food. Most parents who start businesses, or invent products, usually have a similar story of searching online for a product or service, owing to the fact that they were unable to find anything suitable, then to go on to create it themselves.

This is my story exactly, as I was searching for a neat way to defrost all those tiny portions of food I had made for Lilly-Jo, without using a microwave, which seemed about the only option going. Given that I've never owned a microwave and wasn't planning to, I figured I needed some sort of special pan to use over a saucepan, much like an egg-poacher, but made from metal and not plastics. I don't like the idea of plastics leaching chemicals into food, so the challenge was on to create something simple that would work.

I guess the hard part, after I'd made the decision to start a business, was figuring out how on earth to do it. I certainly didn't have any higher education degrees I could call on, and my only business experience to date was manufacturing skateboard decks in my dad's workshop when I was thirteen.

That business actually ran quite successfully for a few months until some of the bigger kids in town bought them and promptly snapped them in half. I figured if I was going to spend my weekends making these things, and then having to issue refunds by Wednesday, I should probably look for an alternative to making pocket money.

Getting back to the task at hand, though, it is really quite daunting when you want to start your own business; basically because you simply don't know where to start. One of the first things I did was to attend a business course, run by a great organisation called Enterprise Nation. I don't mind giving them a plug. If you're in the UK I highly recommend going along to one of their sessions. They also give you a great booklet on how to start a business, which pretty much became my bible for a few months.

I also attended a special course at the British Library on how to be successful in business. It was run by a hot-shot business mentor called Kerrie Dorman, and afterwards she was nice enough to give me her email after which I then proceeded to annoy her with questions for the next year. We seemed to have a good deal going. I always forgot she normally charges money for mentoring, and she always forgot to bill me for her time. That's not to say everyone you ask will love your idea and help.

I remember getting connected to the CEO of one of the biggest baby food brands in the world to showcase my idea. Now, I never had any particular interest in his company as it was purely commercial baby food and I was only dealing with homemade baby food, but I knew I was lucky to be able to converse with him. He pretty much told me, however, that he didn't think the idea was very good, and that I shouldn't pursue it any further. It was a little disappointing, but to be fair, I just took it on the chin. We were clearly two people with a different idea of what our babies should be eating. I have no issues at all with feeding our little ones commercial food every now and then, but as we found out when they have developed a taste for homemade fare, they generally won't tolerate packet mix.

Getting back to the subject though, I think the best thing you can do when you're starting a business is ask questions, even if the answer you get isn't the one you want. Over the course of the last few years I must have asked a hundred people a thousand questions, and I've paid attention to every single answer and used it accordingly. I wish I had written a list of all the things I had to do to start my business. There were so many obstacles and things I had to learn, I think I've kind of blocked it out now. Over the course of the six months it took to set it up I don't think I saw a pillow until 2am any night of the week.

Dealing with clients and manufacturers in different time zones; designing prototypes; patents; trademarks; websites; business bankers; insurance agents; graphic designers; accountants; lawyers and professional photographers...Oh, the list goes on and on, and it was extremely daunting at times, especially when I did pretty much all of it by myself. However, I was lucky to have an extremely good sourcing agent who found me a great company overseas to make my product. There's no way I could have done that by myself. Sometimes you have to know when to spend money to make money, and I'd have paid him double for what he did for me.

As I said earlier I'd wanted to do this for ages but never quite found the motivation. I'm fairly sure it would have been a lot easier if I hadn't had a young family, but that was the real motivation. It's not necessarily that I wanted to create something for them, or to even make money. It was more about doing it to prove to myself that I could do it, and to set an example for them that you can do anything you set your mind to it. Kids learn way more by your example and your actions than they ever will from you telling them to do something. I also have a close group of dad friends who have started their own businesses as well. Some of them have already made a big success of their business while some are just getting started. What they all have in common is that none of them really had any experience in business before they started, and they all had young families when they did take the plunge.

It's been super exciting for me to watch them grow, and even though we are all selling different things, I always look at it as a mildly competitive thing, and always try and be more inventive and successful so I don't lag behind. I want them to succeed as well. So where am I with everything now? Well I guess I've gotten Lillypots to the point where it runs fairly well without me, at least in my getting to bed before midnight.

I still work hard on it every day after the kids are in bed, but the groundwork I put in is solid, and it sells well on Amazon in a variety of countries around the world. I'm always aware that I need to promote it every day, and when you're dealing with your own money, it does give you that extra motivation. I'm lucky to still have a great stable 9-5 job, working for a great company with people I like. But having my own business really lets me experience a different kind of satisfaction that you just don't get working for someone else.

So don't spend years putting things off. If you have a great idea, or even just a mildly good one, ask yourself these questions just as I did: WHY? WHY NOT? WHY NOT ME? WHY NOT NOW? I hope the answer is YES! Good luck!

The Hardest Thing About Being A Daddy

*The dagger hurts a little more
when they take turns twisting it.*

There are all manner of things you can do to prepare and educate yourself about rapidly approaching fatherhood. Almost none of it though, will prepare you for the real thing.

My first born, Lilly-Jo, didn't arrive until I was in my late thirties. I guess that's a bit later in life than the average. I felt very ready for it though, and I was confident. Until I met my wife a few years prior, I experienced nearly a decade of roaming the globe, and flitting in and out of London whenever I needed to work for my next trip. By the time I was settled and married in 2011, I was very excited at the prospect of starting a family. Turns out I didn't have to wait too long. About nine months and three days after the ceremony, I found myself in the delivery room with my wife and what can only be described as the smallest, loudest, most beautiful object I'd ever held. Life was forever changed—but I was ready; right?

So, was I really prepared? Well, yes of course I was or at least I certainly thought so. I had devoured all number of "How to prepare for parenthood" guides. I immersed myself in all of our pre-natal classes to such to a degree that I think all the other dads in the class secretly hated me. Picture that neatly dressed guy with the notepad who always raises his hand first to answer questions and volunteers to be team leader. You know the one. You probably would have hated me too. But that was just how I went about my preparation.

If I were able to press the fast forward button about eight months, you'd have skipped through my dedication to helping out, understanding breastfeeding, taking sole charge of the weaning stage and preparing all of Lilly-Jo's first tastes in food myself. You probably would be thinking; hey, here is a guy who has it covered and nothing is too hard or challenging for him. Believe me, the very hard part of being a father did come...and I was totally unprepared. I am certain that difficult parts will continue to come in waves that I may not ever plan for or expect. For instance, once Lilly-Jo got to a certain age and she became more aware of who was who, in terms of mum and dad, she no longer tolerated me comforting her when she was upset. This was an emotional stretch for me that was very hard to take at times.

I really can't remember when it was that she stopped seeing me as "the" person she wanted in times of distress but I guess it was around the age of twelve months. What made it all the harder for me was that, up until then, she actually preferred me to her mum. Yes, you'll be happy when your baby prefers you over mum too! To add insult to proverbial injury, not only could I no longer go get her from her crib when she awoke crying, she would actually cry more until her mum came and picked her up! I found it both frustrating and sad because I couldn't help Louise any more in the middle of the night. And that little girl whom I used to sing to sleep every night, no longer wanted me in her time of need.

I'm told it's a fairly common thing that happens to dads, and some of my friends have said much the same thing happened to them. While it was definitely the hardest obstacle that I've encountered as a parent, I do know one day it may change back. Lots of parents have told me it will, so I'm very encouraged by that.

Children tend to waffle back and forth in their parental favouritisms without much regard to the pain they may cause us. We have to forgive them and not take it to heart.

I'm sure many of you out there have, or will experience your own tough moments. They may or may not be like mine, but trust me, you'll have something come along that will rock your boat. You need to be prepared for that. When it does come, take it on the chin; it's not personal, you're just watching a little person evolve, and you'll be a better person and father if you don't let it defeat you. Even a few years later, both the kids still gravitate to their mum when they are really upset. It is much better with Lilly-Jo now, and I have accepted that it's nothing personal.

NB: Special thanks to my friend, Travis, for allowing me to use his photo in this chapter. He waited seven years for this moment with his daughter, Haven. It's my favourite image from Instagram.

Don't Live Your Dreams Through Your Kids

*Remember how happy it made
you living your life for someone else?*

I think there is a fine line between being a pushy parent and being an encouraging parent. It's important to encourage your children to discover their full potential. I think some of us, as adults, carry around disappointments and regrets about our own lives. Sure, people say that you shouldn't have regrets, but I don't believe that. It's human nature. I'm sure at least half the people who tell you that they have none are probably fooling themselves. Like it or not, the things that we have, or have not done are experiences that are good things to have sometimes. We need to be reminded about the mistakes we made and the places in life we don't want to be ever again.

I don't necessarily have regrets about the things that I did do, it's more about the things that I didn't do. My biggest, not realising until my late thirties that I was in fact capable of so much more than I gave myself credit for. I'd always dreamed of starting my own business but was never willing to take the risk. I was never sure or confident

that I had the mindset to pull it off, considering I had zero business experience. Suffice to say, I did start a business and it was a reasonable success. It was one of the most challenging things I've ever done and I'll probably always regret that I didn't do it five years earlier. I have to wear that every day and I just can't help but think about what could have been if I'd done it sooner. Still, though, everything I did, or didn't do, has brought me here. It brought me my family and for that, I'm always grateful.

I'm a country kid who lives in the city, and it was important for me that my kids share a part of what I had growing up, as selfish as that might sound. When Lilly-Jo was born I was filled with hope that she might share my love of the ocean and surfing. Because I love it, I want her to love it too. But mostly, I wanted her to love the outdoors. I will never forget the first time I pushed her into a wave while she was lying on my surfboard. She was around two at the time and it was a rather spontaneous decision; she waded into the shallows and asked to try it. This was unusual for her as she is normally very apprehensive about new activities. As you might imagine, I was propelled into such a state of excitement by her enthusiasm that I immediately placed her on the board and pushed her into a very small wave. She floated easily towards her mum who was standing on the sand. And for those few seconds, as I watched her glide gently to the shore, it was the happiest moment of my life.

The joy of the moment changed very quickly when the board stopped and she tipped over the side. Even though the water level was only just over ankle deep, she got a face full of sea water, much to her horror, and Louise had to pluck her out and comfort her.

I'll fast forward past the massive telling off I got—it was extensive, believe me, and I totally deserved it. Moving on then, to the biggest disappointment that ensued from the affair. Poor Lilly-Jo was so shaken up by the whole thing that she refused to go into the water again for the rest of the vacation. It was a double blow to the gut and the heart for me. Not only had I let myself down in the safety stakes, but also I had probably put her off the ocean for the rest of her life.

This bone-headed move reminded me of the years growing up when my own dad really wanted me to be involved in sailing down at the local yacht club. Although I had sailed for a few years, took some pride in it and even won a few times, I never really liked it. I was really happy, and relieved if you want to know the truth, when it came to an end. I have not set foot on a yacht ever since. I guess I just wanted to do my own thing and I know I will have to recognise that Lilly-Jo and Huey will probably be the same. I want them to aim high in life and not hold themselves back like I did, be it in their careers or interests.

I will always try and introduce them to the activities I like, but I already know there is now a clear line in the sand as to how far I am going to push them. While I'll always endeavour to be a part of the things they like doing, it's OK to hope they might enjoy some of the things that I like just as much.

You might have noticed I haven't touched on influencing a child when it comes to their chosen career path. A wise man once told me that in this modern day, it's fairly pointless to navigate your child's career path from a young age. It's not that it's a bad thing to do, rather it's because technology is moving so fast that you can't predict what kinds of jobs there will be in twenty years' time. If you have hopes that at least one of your children might follow your career path or enter into the family business, there is a good chance by the time that moment comes that career may not be an option anymore. The best you can do is to encourage their interests and develop their street smarts. My goal is to have kids who do well in school of course, but I want them to be adaptable as well. Children with a good sense of self-worth and solid confidence can deal with anything that life throws at them.

In the end, the most important thing for them is to enjoy whatever path they choose. As parents it's vital for us to help keep their options open and offer them a wide variety of directions in life. I'm sure my kids might make some wrong decisions, but at least they will make those decisions themselves and not have me make them for them. Hopefully then they will use those experiences to make better decisions. Generally though, as the saying goes; *life is what happens when you're making plans*—and there are no truer words spoken.

Show Me The Boy At Seven And I'll Show You The Man

They really should mention this before you leave the hospital.

Believe it or not, I met Louise in a nightclub, way back in 2007. I can be a little antisocial at times but I'm fairly fearless when I really want to meet people. So when I spotted this lovely lady across the bar, looking ever so unobtainable, I just walked straight up to her and said hello. I typically try to find common ground very quickly when meeting people but not in a mundane way. I quickly discovered that she was a psychologist—which was brilliant because I always fancied myself as a bit of an amateur one.

Obviously, seeking to try to impress her, I recalled all my learnings from that behavioural science class I took back in college. Most of the babbling I did centred around the argument of nature vs. nurture, and which has a more profound effect on a person's outcome

growing up. It's a fascinating topic and she was clearly impressed with my intellect, or at least she did a fine job of pretending she was.

Moving on to the actual subject of this chapter, whether or not you believe a person is shaped more by nature or by nurture; it's generally accepted that a child of seven, for better or worse, is fundamentally the person that they will always be. While the distinction between the two isn't always certain, it's clear that your child will inherit many of your characteristics simply by default. It was painfully obvious to Louise that Lilly-Jo had inherited quite a lot of my personality. You see, Lilly-Jo can be really anti-social at times, despite my best efforts to hide that side of my persona from her. She also shares her mother's stubborn gene quite strongly as well. Can you guess how thrilled I was with that unexpected extra?

One of the more interesting traits Lilly-Jo was born with, that no one is able to understand, is her reluctance to try new tasks until she processes them and believes in her mind that she can do them. This was evident in her reluctance to crawl and also to walk. We estimate she spent less than an hour on her tummy as a baby due to the fact that she absolutely hated it. She also walked late at fourteen months (this was brilliant though, as no matter where we left her, she never moved) and went from nothing to running in just a few weeks. It was as if she was waiting until she really thought she could do it. Granted, this trait can be a little frustrating for me at times as it limits the things I can do with her and our activities can be very repetitive. I worry a little that this reluctance to try new things for fear of failing isn't really a good trait to take through life.

As we all know, you have to be bad at something first before you can be any good at it. So I've taken it upon myself to really encourage her (I won't say push) into physical activities that she wouldn't normally try. The playground has been the perfect place for that and I've gradually coaxed her out of her shell and she's quite the little daredevil now. She still has that super cautious side and you can always see that behind her eyes. I just hope that when she starts school that it will have all paid off. We want her to enjoy trying new sports or activities and not avoid them because she thinks they're too hard.

I wish I had a more definitive answer to the question of nature v nurture but I don't think even our white-cloaked scientific friends really know which side has more of a direct effect on the growing infant. Without wanting to generalise, but to be anecdotal here, when I look around I see more and more kids growing up with insecurities that just didn't seem to exist when I was young.

Body shaming, coming from the mass media's influence, is one thing that causes insecurities and it targets girls more than it does boys. I'm painfully aware of this because I have a girl. I also believe that, owing to the hectic lives of families with both parents working, that kids sometimes do feel a bit neglected and insecure. I think about all the people I knew growing up who weren't the nicest kids, and realise that they were probably just insecure. People with insecurities tend to be the ones who belittle or verbally berate others simply to make themselves feel better. It might be a pretty basic way to sum up a trait but I think it's usually fairly accurate.

So for me personally, it's about taking the approach that when it's nature vs. nurture, it's a 50/50 draw. I think that's the only way I can really look at it. I'm happy when I see good traits and behaviours come out in my kids, but when I see bad ones, I move to knock it on the head as soon as possible (the behaviour not the kid) and steer them towards a better path. Children definitely aren't born with an inherited ability to be kind, loyal, or have good moral fibre. Sure, they might be born with a predisposition for all of those things but it's something you have to nurture and develop.

I hope that the work we are putting into our kids early on pays off in the long run. I hope like me, you don't want to leave too much up to chance. I want to summarise the chapter by saying this... Raising kids can be tough and although at times the days seem long, the years are short. I really hope you recognise that and understand that when you're watching your child blow out their 7th birthday candles, you're witnessing, for the most part, a fully-formed person.

This is why it's so important to really put in as much effort as you can in the early days of child raising. I treat every hour and every interaction as an opportunity to build the best little people I can. Seeing as I made them, it's my responsibility, and every day counts. Make your days the same. If you do, the future rewards will make it all worthwhile.

When I Was A Boy

My iPad was a BMX bike.

There is no escaping the fact that we are living in a fast-paced world these days and that causes massive strains on our time and our finances, especially for families. Just for a reference, I'm 41 years old; so back when I was a kid in the 80s, I'd watch shows like the Jetsons on Saturday morning. I remember how they used to use video watches to call each other and I remember thinking, *there's no way that could ever happen in real life*. Fast-forward to today and those Jetsons' video watches, or facetime, as we call it, are just a normal part of life.

Forgive my slight detour down memory lane but I had a very happy childhood and I feel very comfortable saying that. Everyone's recollection of growing up is different, but as I was a bit of a country bumpkin before I moved to London, I see a contrast between the material possessions kids have, compared to what I had (or didn't have) growing up. Even though we didn't have all the tech gadgets that kids have today, my brother and I were lucky to have both parents under the same roof. I know that there are so many young kids out there now who come from single parent families, and there are times I feel guilty and sad about that. While we didn't live in a large bustling city, our town was just perfect for us.

Up until about 1998, big cities were fairly unknown to me and I thought visiting Hobart, which is the capital of Tasmania, was a bit of a thrill! The hustle and bustle of it all was truly shocking to me, coming from a town of barely five thousand people. At the time, Hobart probably had about fifty thousand residents, on a good day!

Exploring that city was an adventure, and all the entertainment and things to do were just mind-boggling to a kid. Where I grew up, we didn't have all the trappings that big cities have to thrill and entertain children. We were largely, but safely, left on our own to play and amuse ourselves. From what I remember, that usually involved a lot of bike riding and exploring adventures. I can say that I enjoyed a childhood where providing my own entertainment was a bit of a requirement. You probably know that old adage "Necessity is the mother of invention" right? Well my brother and I were really good at inventing lots of things to keep us busy.

Setting off in the morning on my bike to a friend's house across town, then returning home just before dark was an adventure in itself, and these are some of my most enduring memories of my childhood. It wasn't that we didn't have toys or other material things—we had them, but even so, I distinctly remember being less interested in them when the sun was shining. Having my kids doing that same sort of thing, considering where we live in central London, is almost impossible. Another unfortunate thing in this modern age is the fact that children aren't left to rely on their imaginations, or simple things such as wooden spoons or sticks, for play and recreation.

I can't help but notice the amount of money that parents spend on their kids, compared to what my parents spent. It's often a seemingly endless supply of expensive toys and electronic goods that rotate through children's lives. Sometimes I wonder if a lot of these things are purchased to alleviate the (possible) guilt parents may have for not being able to spend all the time they can with their kids. Since having kids, I've really noticed the difference in family dynamics from when I was little. Today, people seem to have very long and crazy hours at work. Young babies or toddlers are very often looked after by nannies or spend five days a week in nursery. These times are tough for families and in many cases, both parents work purely out of necessity. I understand that.

I wish more parents would realise that an endless supply of material gifts isn't something that's useful for kids. The time that you do get to spend with your kids is best used encouraging them to be creative and to develop their imaginations with play. It's one of the best ways to enhance a child's emotional and intellectual growth, and it's why I constantly engage Lilly-Jo and Huey in play that doesn't involve many props or toys. Remember that for me, this only equates to a few hours a day through the week, but I do make the most of every minute of that short time.

I invent imaginary characters for both of my kids all the time, and Lilly-Jo, at least, also invents her own characters. She gets so much more enjoyment from these play times than she does opening a present. I am sure there will come a time when it will become more and more difficult to keep the material trappings from her, especially when all the other kids at school have them. Hopefully, we will have developed her imagination and self-sufficiency skills enough for her not to see these things as necessities.

What I truly want to avoid is the silent family syndrome. I don't want to be a family whose kids have their faces buried in electronics and no one talks to each other. It's sad, and no good can come from raising kids that way. However, I know not to judge when I see that scenario because you never know the full story. Maybe the parents were just frazzled that day and needed the kids to zone out for bit. I've been there, done that, on occasion too.

This is just my opinion and one I hold onto tightly. I'm allowed to express it here because, well, it is my book (wry smile). I'm sure you have your own ideas about how to raise kids in these modern times. Just make sure you step outside of it once in a while and take yourself back to your own childhood to see how it matches up. It just seems so much more complicated these days to be a kid when it really need not be . I'm not sure there is any magic formula for raising a happy well-adjusted child but I'm fairly sure the latest video watch probably won't play much of a positive part in that. Unless of course they wear it into their teenage years and it has a tracking device embedded in it. I could see that being a very useful gadget for parents the world over.

Life Advice, Part 2

Dear Huey,

I always recount with great joy my own brother's (Uncle Telen) upbringing as the second child just like you are.

When I was born my mother, your Nanny Pam, documented my entire early life in a detailed logbook. Everything I ate and every hour I slept, it was all there; such was the devotion shown to me. When your Uncle Telen came along three years later, it appears he had no such book dedicated to him. No one is really sure why, not even your Nanny although I suspect it was really down to time, or the lack of it.

While I try not to upset your uncle with this fact, it's often hard not to remind him of the absence of said book, especially around Xmas time. I'm also afraid to say it's a similar case with you, not because we chose not to do one, but simply because it was very time consuming having a new born and a three year old. It just wasn't possible. We were a bit more skilled as parents by the time you came along so we relied on our knowledge a lot more.

Getting back to your Uncle Telen though, I used to like to steal your Grandma's phone and send him a text simply saying, "You were adopted". It's pretty cruel, I know, but it's just the way siblings

are and I'm sure you'll have your own fun and games with your big sister in years to come.

Like your sister before you, there was much fanfare at your arrival. You were a whopper of a baby at nine pounds and your mother did an amazing job during your delivery. The anaesthetist in charge of pain relief on the ward that day somehow managed not to attach your mum's epidural properly, so she had a completely drug free birth. All I can say is that if you're ever mad at your mum over the course of your life, try and remember what she went through bringing you into the world. It was quite a feat of endurance and courage.

If I am totally honest with you, I was very excited to be having a boy. I think with your sister there was a little less pressure on me because, well, I'm not a girl and I wasn't expected to know what being one felt like. With you though, it was like suddenly having a mini-me, and for better or worse I knew what the ups and downs of what it was going to be like being you. Some things scared me about that; some things I'm glad about. When you were born it indeed felt like looking in the mirror of time a bit, I guess you could say. You were everything your mother and I could have hoped for. A strong, robust little man you were, and somehow able to pretty much stand by yourself (with minimal support) at two and a half months of age; quite a quirk of nature.

You were also a very good looking little fellow and I'm sure this will become very useful when your sister starts bringing home her friends, and you can play the cute little brother role to perfection. Just as in your sister's letter in this book, we want you to live your life to the fullest and not be held back by anyone else's ideas, including those of your parents.

I would dearly love to find something that we can enjoy doing together and over time I will introduce you to all the things I love to do. You can pick and choose what you like or come up with your own ideas of fun things we can do. As with your sister I care not what these things are. It's only important that you find them and do them, hopefully inviting me along every once in a while to share them with you. Your mother and I learned so much with your sister and we intend to apply all these learnings into making your life as great as possible; that, I can assure you.

I actually started writing this book just before you were born and finished it when you were about six months old. So, if you're reading it, and wondering why your sister has the bulk of the pages, then realise it was just because you were a little young for me to know as much about you as I did about her.

Speaking of her, I'm sure you will have your ups and downs as brother and sister, but let me assure you there was no one happier and prouder than her the day you were born. She was thrilled, besotted, and very protective of her little brother. Your mother and I hope very much that you'll always be there for each other and that you'll watch over her when you get bigger, just as she did for you.

I like to think that I'm a very open and forward-thinking dad and, if your mother had let me have a study, then the door would always have been open to you and your sister to talk to me about anything you wanted to. In the end I had to settle for the kitchen, which is where you'll find me most nights, cooking you something delicious. So stop by often—even if it's just because you're hungry. I'm always there to listen.

Love Dad

PS this photo was taken when I took you to my work for the first time.

What To Expect When You Propose

By the time your bended knee straightens, the wedding venue will be booked.

Now that I'm a veteran in the field of proposing (one proposal makes you a veteran), I'm of the firm belief that engagement rings should come with a small label that says; "Caution, may cause wedding". You see, I hadn't even thought ahead to an actual wedding! When I decided to propose to Louise all I was really thinking about was the proposal, and I most certainly hadn't given any thought to the wedding itself.

Let me re-phrase; the idea that a wedding would occur due to this proposal never even entered my mind. For me, it was merely an expression of my commitment to her. I just naively assumed that a wedding would come along by itself, as in the next few years when we were ready. I've since discovered, through my own experiences and also through that of friends, that proposals winding up

as lengthy engagements most certainly are not the norm, by quite a margin.

I feel like I should continue to explain what I mean, so here goes. Most men like me start out with the best of intentions when it comes to proposing to their loved ones. Careful thought and considerable expense is put into the jewellery aspect, parents are consulted, and appropriate venues are chosen for the bended knee thing that you (should) customarily do. Engagements are events that change our lives as couples and are truly lovely affairs, even if they don't go perfectly as planned, they will always be remembered fondly.

I thought the best way to illustrate this was to simply share my engagement story, as it was immensely joyous in every way. To be honest though, the tornado-pace that the wedding preparations moved at, in the hours and days following the big proposal, were a bit of a shock. I proposed to Louise on a picturesque hilltop in Biarritz, France. I figured if she said no I could always just jump off into the watery abyss of the ocean below. Luckily, of course, she said yes. There were many tears, and even Louise cried a bit too.

At this fleeting point in life, you may actually be the closest you will ever be. If there is anything really important you need to say, say it then and say it loud. Your partner will be listening as never before (or ever again, likely) and will always remember the moment and the words. From memory, I told her that it was very important that we didn't live our lives under the constraints of anyone else's and she agreed. I've never followed the rules of society or anyone's ideas about what I can or cannot do. This wasn't going to be any different.

After the euphoria of the proposal, the phone calls started. I swear they went on for hours, and after her phone battery died, she started using mine. Mums and dads, aunties, uncles and friends; all were called and so loud were the shrieked responses that I swear she had it on speaker-phone. These calls continued for many, many days afterwards. We couldn't go anywhere unless we were sure that electricity was available for charging of our phones.

Once the calls subsided to a manageable stream, along came the start of...the lists. Oh, the lists! I still remember them. The first one was for the bridesmaid—obviously very important. Then there was a list for prospective wedding guests, and this, this is when it really dawned on me that there was going to be an actual wedding. It wasn't that I was scared. It was just, as I said previously, that I hadn't considered that there was going to be a wedding.

This reminds me of our friends, Veronica and John. John proposed at about 3am at a wedding they were attending in Veronica's hometown in Spain. Apparently, it was tradition that all the girls in their family get married in the local church. Not surprisingly, at around 9am the next morning, running on zero sleep, he found himself at the foot of said church discussing possible wedding dates. He was still shell shocked when I saw him a few weeks later! I put my hand on his shoulder and gave him that look that said, "I've been there too buddy, don't worry everything is going to be fine." I have to say that one of the best things about wedding preparations is the excitement that the bride-to-be feels. It made me feel happy seeing Louise so happy to make plans and preparations for our wedding.

We were married a little over a year after the proposal and it was a very nice, though chaotic time in the lead-up. There wasn't a second wasted, as far as I could see, and I lost track of how many times she fell asleep in bed with a bridal magazine. This leads me to offering some advice concerning how much of a role you should play in the wedding preparations. If you're anything like me, you have no clue about colour-coordination, or other necessities of wedding venue style and décor, so it was carefully decided that I should play a more background role. I did make myself available when it came time to select the caterers, and of course, I made certain that I had a nice suit, tailored to her preference. Basically, all I had to do really was turn up on the day. No, wait, I did do one very important thing and that, my friends, was choosing the wedding beer! That was brilliant and I was thrilled to be given *carte blanche*.

So what I'm trying to tell you is to think a little past the actual proposal event and be prepared to get caught up in the excitement of it all. I don't want to sound too stereotypical here but many women have thought about their wedding day since they were little girls. It's important for you to be nothing less than super-support-ive. After all, you started this whole thing!

There is however one golden rule that overrides all other rules when it comes to wedding preparations. When the groom is asked anything, say, "yes" to everything. It's the only advice you ever need to know. And one more thing, when on your stag (bachelor party), don't get too carried away. Always follow the law, especially when you're on your stag do and you have all your mates telling you that the police will give you a free pass for that lapse in judgement. There are no free passes!

Becoming A Role Model

As if being a new dad isn't enough pressure.

Two things will happen instantaneously on the day your baby is born. One you will definitely notice, but the other, probably not so much. First thing to happen, you become a dad, and that is fairly obvious. The second thing is that you become a role model as well. I didn't realise it at the time that I would have two very important roles that are separate but entirely intertwined. It was probably for the best that I remained unaware as now that I know I need to be a role model, I'm honestly more daunted by that!

When we were expecting our first baby all I really wanted was to have a healthy child. However if I'm straight up, I'll admit that I was secretly hoping for a boy. Most parents do secretly wish that their child would be one gender or the other. I will tell you that there was no rational reason for my wanting to have a son, only that I was a boy myself and well, I pretty much know how we function. So naturally it should be easier to raise someone of your own gender, I thought to myself. I guess men imagine all kinds of scenarios as the due date looms ever closer and as we decided not to find out the gender of our first baby, the picture I created in my head was that of a mini-me. Don't get me wrong; I was never disappointed to have a girl though, far from it.

The moment Lilly-Jo popped out we bonded very quickly. I looked to the heavens and was thankful for the ten fingers and ten toes that I saw in front of me. What happened, weirdly enough, immediately after the birth was that I became partially undaunted about becoming a dad, especially to a girl. In a way, there was a slight relief because even though I was going to be raising a daughter, there were a lot of things that I didn't know, and may never truly know, about what it's like to be a girl. So I rightly, or wrongly, convinced myself that Louise would understand our baby better and could always direct me in certain areas. It was a bit of a crazy notion I suppose but maybe it was just a coping mechanism. We men are famous for those.

That notion, however, went right out the window pretty quickly in the first few days after the birth when we realised that no one had the slightest idea what was going on. It made no difference what gender our baby was as there was little or no distinction, other than that one can pee in your face and one can't, and that's about as bluntly as I can put it. I guess this time period, in the days and weeks postpartum, was when I really decided to step up a gear and I began my transformation in trying to be the best role model I could be. To me, the most important thing you need to realise as a dad is that your job as a role model starts on day one. Just because your baby can't talk and it may not seem like they are really taking things in doesn't mean they aren't. Most behaviours, and the bulk of your child's personality, is formed in the first seven years of life.

This isn't something I made up; it's generally regarded as fact that the first seven years are crucial. Our white-coated friends who love to study these types of things, have found this to be so. Now, seven years might sound like a long time to you but trust me it's not. You'll hear it said over and over again how fast it moves. You, too, will undoubtedly find yourself saying just how fast time flies and how quickly kids grow. I find myself staring down the barrel of Lilly-Jo's 4th birthday and wondering how on earth that came around so fast? It still seems like yesterday when she was born.

It's difficult in some ways to understand your influence over your own child because the things that help shape them are taken in and absorbed over their entire childhood, and in such small increments. There is rarely a defining moment when you notice the fruits of your tenure as role model. This is true of almost all kids and all family situations, except when it comes to cursing. There is a special cursing antenna that every child must be born with, you will learn! Kids can hear a curse word through two thick walls while playing underneath a bed and miraculously, they will instantly be able to repeat the word and possibly even spell it. They may become specifically adept at repeating the word to grandparents or other prominent people around you. You've been warned.

The most important aspect to recognise about being a role model is that everyone has different ideas about what that should involve, even the parents of the same child. It's no use having me, or anyone else, explaining to you what you should be doing; it's your right to raise your child however you see fit. Nevertheless, it doesn't hurt to keep an open mind about how you go about your new role, because you can always pick up on things that other parents do. I've done this a lot, especially in public playgroup situations. Sometimes you see very small interactions between other parents and children that you'll like and want to mimic, and this is a good thing.

I have to admit that I do tend to judge others, not how they treat the people they know but more in the way they treat the people they don't. I dislike it when people are rude to staff in restaurants or other public places, and my kids will never see me doing that. I hope that when they see my interactions that they learn that being "served" by someone means you use your pleases and thankyous, just as you would in your own home or when at a friend's house. Generally though, when it comes to interactions, there is a difference between being polite and being a pushover. This can sometimes be difficult to define. I know that my kids will encounter many an irate fellow human. As I have learned and as I will teach them, 99% of the time it's better to just walk away from something.

Or, if it's a superficial road-related altercation, drive away with perhaps a few consecutive blows on your car's horn, for example.

I'd like to teach them that while it's important to stand their ground, often very little is gained by getting all puffy and red faced. In parenting, sometimes too much importance is placed on verbalising or instructing your child when it comes to shaping the way you want them to act. Children, especially of a younger age, tend to mimic those around them before their personalities are fully-formed. So what they see you do, they will take as normal and copy. Trying to shape a well-balanced child with purely verbal instruction alone is a bit like giving them a blank storybook and asking them to act out the plot. Every interaction they see you undertake, from the guy in the gas station to the door-to-door salesman, will all go in their heads and be processed then filed away. So sometimes, even when life (and temper) is screaming at you to act a certain way, you've got to do the opposite if you're with your kids.

When it comes to kids and forming their personalities, talk is cheap, especially given in an instructional form. Most of what goes into making them is based on what they see around them every minute of every day. One thing I remember my parents telling me was to never discuss religion or politics with friends. It took me a long time to really understand what they meant by that, but I totally get it now. I've learned that this wisdom means that personal beliefs shouldn't be a defining factor in friendships. I can't say that I haven't been outspoken about my beliefs, but I do try and not let that define me.

I want my kids to grow up knowing that you don't have to surround yourself with likeminded people in order to feel comfortable or secure. I want them to grow up seeing diversity as a good thing and encourage them to have a wide range of friendships. While I have my own close group of friends with whom I share the same beliefs, I also have friends outside that core group who are polar opposites. I think it's a good thing having friends who, on paper, would seem like they'd have nothing in common with you, but you just enjoy their company anyway.

By far the most important role your children will see you play is the one you act out every day with their mother. The way you interact with your partner will be, for the most part, how they will see relationships for the rest of their lives. Children are very sensitive to parental interactions from a young age and even though they may not process things the same way you and I do, it all gets absorbed and stored in their brains like water in a sponge. Keep that in mind if a heated "discussion" should ever arise between the two of you in their presence. You can read between the lines on that one. So much lies before us in the world of "role modelling" for us dads. There will be highs and there will certainly be lows, that I can promise you.

What you have in that little person standing in front of you, or being cradled in your arms, is in part an empty book that you can fill with whatever amazing chapters you wish. This is an opportunity to change the things you don't like about yourself, or right the wrongs of your own upbringing, and let go of the past. Seldom in life will you ever get another opportunity quite like it; to be both creator and teacher to a small human is perhaps your most important role and the biggest test you'll undertake. Make the most of that opportunity.

I thought I'd just share my basic ideology about the kind of role model I try to be to my own children. It's really important to me that they learn to treat others with respect and have good manners. It costs you nothing and will get you far in life.

The Struggle Is Real

The struggle is real; very, very real.

Nobody tells you. It's the famous mantra cried out by new parents all around the world every day when faced with the trials and tribulations of raising a child. We know the struggles, but we know the joys too.

I was prepared—or thought I was—so it wasn't strictly true for me, thanks to one simple piece of advice (OK, warning) from my best friend after he had two kids. I figured it wasn't going to be too bad. He said, and I quote, "Some days you won't even have time to go to the bathroom". I remember scoffing at this at the time thinking how ridiculous it sounded. I mean the bathroom, really? Of course we will still use the bathroom. Fast forward through a few years and now I have my own kids. Guess what? My friend was fairly spot on with his advice, if you want to call it advice. Yes, trying to visit the bathroom, or any amenity-styled facility, can be near impossible at times with young children in tow.

It's hard to actually remember all the different scenarios that unfolded over the years to hinder my access but it seems like I've been trying to pee for three years. Take my outing last weekend with Lilly-Jo to the local park, to the shopping mall, and then to eat. We were a little late getting to the mall from the park and she was

getting really hungry. Have you seen those Snickers ads on TV? The ads where the hungry person turns into a stroppy, famous person until they get their snack! Well Lilly-Jo is quite a lot like that—except she's meaner and louder. My little girl gets hangry i.e. hungry and angry. It's not pretty. She won't tolerate hunger at all and regresses back to being some kind of rabid cave-child, complete with wild flailing arms and legs.

It happened just as we were entering the mall, you know what I'm talking about don't you? Lilly-Jo decides she needs to pee so we have to race downstairs to the baby change and ring the attendant to come and open the door. He takes ages to get to the door. It then takes a while for me to sort her out and by this stage, she's going berserk with hunger. By this time, I too need to use the facilities myself but I quickly weigh up whether the thirty seconds I need to pee is going to be the thirty seconds that causes the world to stop turning. If she loses it entirely, due to waiting thirty seconds for me, no restaurant will seat us unless I can guarantee that I have arm restraints and sedatives for her!

The struggle is also well documented when it comes to leaving the house on an excursion. It used to be that when we wanted to leave the house, we generally only needed to grab a set of keys and we were off. Now that we have kids, just leaving the house to stroll to the park might as well be a day trip to Mt Everest, considering what goods and essentials need to be organised and packed. Bottles, pacifiers, diapers, as well as military-style scheduling, all need to be considered and if you are missing just one item or piece of information, disaster threatens on the horizon.

Let me warn you of another common struggle, the struggle with Number 2. Kids and babies have a knack for picking the most inappropriate times to do Number 2s. I know they don't do it on purpose, but their timing is always spot-on! We found that the moment is generally as soon as we had locked the front door to leave and not a moment sooner. The looming Number 2 forces you to march your lovely cherubs back inside and change them. This is a one-two punch on many occasions as quite often when Lilly-Jo was still a baby, she would see going back into the house as a cue to start feeding again. So not only have you ended up back in the house but also you're back inside watching your wife feed the kids again.

It's kind of a bit like the Groundhog Day movie, but without all the extra characters or truck delivering money at the bank, that over the course of a few days you can easily work out how to steal. Speaking of trucks, let's talk about cars. Cars either become your greatest ally, or the biggest adversary you have when you have kids. The hardest thing I found was the limited amount of time a child will sit happily in them. I talked it over with a few people and we all seemed to concur that you have about two hours to get from point A to B before things, and by things I mean your baby or toddler, starts to lose their calm and sweet attitude.

Unfortunately, given that we live in central London, there isn't much worth driving to that is less than two hours away. You can imagine our drives were (and continue to be) fairly white-knuckled rides as we both hoped and prayed we could get to where we were going without too much drama. Don't be discouraged though, we did have some brilliant trips. Most of these revolved around when Lilly-Jo would fall asleep as soon as we set off and wake up as soon as we arrived. Truth be told, these trips were few and far between.

A typical drive consisted of spending the whole trip trying to coax her off to sleep so she would arrive at the in-laws, or wherever we were off to, fresh and happy. Of course she never heard about resistance being futile. She could resist the whole way and fall into a deep slumber as soon as we pulled into their drive.

Car trips and shopping malls and Number 2s aside, not everything I thought would be a struggle turned out to be. Air travel turned out to be a dream-scenario when it came to Lilly-Jo. For some reason the G-force of the take-off would put her into the deepest, most peaceful slumber that a parent only dreams about. Each time and without fail, she would be out like a light before the plane had barely gotten one hundred feet off the ground. I swear to you if

I could have bought a device that would have had the same effect at home during bedtime, I would have bankrupted myself to purchase it.

You see, the most important thing I've learned about the struggle is not to fight it. It's fruitless. Unless you are Lilly-Jo, resistance is indeed futile. You'll never win against it. There are just too many variables stacked against you. I generally just try and go with the flow and throw the proverbial clock out the window. If we get there we get there and if we don't, at least we tried.

For me, a successful day with the kids is having them both still alive at the end of it, and a cold beer in my hand; the details are simply incidental.

2015

January	February	March

April	May	June

July	August	September

October	November	December

It's all about Lilly-Jo

AU
PETIT CAFE

baby

boy

is

here

the
Mulberry
Tel: 01428 644460
www.themulberryinn.co.uk

niche
ignite
www.nicheignite.com

LIST

broccoli
mushrooms
chocolate
cheese
tomato paste
tortilla
pasta
prosecco
coffee
wine

lollipop

The Second Coming

*The first baby takes up 100% of your time;
you've got nothing to lose by making baby #2*

I can honestly say that I never experienced any kind of apprehension or nerves when Louise was pregnant with Lilly-Jo. While I think I coped pretty well with the first few years of child raising, you're never really fully prepared for the sheer amount of time that you must invest. I don't think anyone is.

We were very spoiled with our first baby, Lilly-Jo. For the first six months of her life, she was what people describe as a "dream baby". She was born naturally with a little help from one of those suction cup *thingies* they use to pull babies out when needed. I always forget what they're called. I always described her birth as fairly straightforward, when you consider all the heart breaking things that can go wrong during birth. I am forever grateful that she arrived in a good state.

You may not believe it but our little one was also very quick to get herself into a nice feeding schedule, which is every parent's dream. She would feed from Mummy then pass out for three hours then awake to feed again. You could set your watch by her and it was very satisfying. You can also imagine our sheer delight when at just three months of age, she started sleeping soundly through the night. I can't explain the sheer elation that a baby sleeping through the night brings a parent! Once, she even slept in until 11am, on a Sunday! Oh we were smug; oh so smug.

Don't worry though, this all ended very abruptly at around eight months of age when our perfect baby started waking constantly throughout the night, screaming blue murder. I was convinced that someone had switched her for a look-a-like. Where had that peaceful little thing gone and why was she suddenly so angry at the world? This pattern of waking in the early hours slowly improved, but even now, at three years old, she is still partial to a good old shriek at 3am. We have adjusted and now, it's just a part of our lives. It's amazing how you adapt to broken sleep.

Let me be open and honest about the fact that I was, understandably, nervous about us having another baby, and I did take some convincing. It was never a question of whether or not I wanted another baby but more that I was completely daunted by how we would cope with two. Louise's main principle was that she didn't want Lilly-Jo to grow up alone and having a sibling meant she would always have someone close to her once we had long gone. She was an only child for a very long time before she had two half-sisters and a brother who came along. I know she experienced something that I never felt, and being an only child can sometimes be a bit lonely.

We did talk it over quite a lot and eventually decided that we would try for another one. I would highly recommend having this talk with your partner. I must say I did find it hard when she mistook my apprehension as reluctance, which it wasn't really. It was more my being over-cautious, but that's just the way I am. I can also remember in one of our pre-birth conversations telling Louise that there was no way on earth we would get another easy going baby. What we did indeed get was a baby so different from Lilly-Jo that I swear they're not related. Funnily enough, about nine months and a few days after that final conversation we were blessed with a little boy to add to our family. Secretly, I'd always worried that my love for beer might have left my *swimmers* a bit sea sick, but clearly this was not the case.

He is, of course, a lovely little boy and for the most part a healthy one. Born at nine pounds he was a bit of a thumper and his love of feeding was most evident right from day one. Unfortunately, he suffers from every parent's worst nightmare, which is the dreaded colic. I hope you never have to experience it. I'm not even going to bother telling you what the medical definition of colic is, instead I'll tell you what happens. Huey basically screams all night and it's so sad because there is little you can do other than comfort him. Despite trying a few different solutions nothing has really made much difference. We are basically a household full of overtired zombies. It's been very hard. It's not his fault, though, poor thing, and we are doing our best to help him. I pray for the day when his tummy rights itself and he can rest peacefully, and our ears can stop ringing.

I've learned when you're struggling, you shouldn't fight the struggle, and I mentioned that philosophy in a previous chapter. Even though it's hard to follow my own advice, I do know that this stage will pass soon and he will be a happier baby. As far as my advice on having a second baby goes, you should go for it. One is the loneliest number, you know. I do caution you again, to make sure you and your partner talk about it first, a lot! Don't worry about the prospect of not having the means to cope with two little ones either. Your first child takes up a hundred percent of your time anyway; you've got nothing to lose!

NB: I just wanted to add as an update that we ended up having some remarkable success treating Huey's colic. We followed the advice of friends and turned to our local chiropractor. While it didn't seem an obvious choice, it really made a huge difference. I'm not really into handing out medical advice but if your baby is suffering from colic, I recommend looking into it!

17 Things Not To Do When Your Partner Is Pregnant

Try not to laugh, these things really happened.

origdesilou: Desiree, California, USA – His stupid fantasy football and fantasy baseball league was by far my biggest annoyance. He would spend hours researching players and arranging his line up during my pregnancy and even worse he found time to trade players during labor. He even managed to draft a player during our honeymoon. lol

february.fox: I was induced with my first and wasn't allowed to eat while in labor waiting for baby. Hubby said, "no worries! I'm going through this with you. You don't eat, I won't eat"…10 mins later he ordered a huge sub sandwich and later pizza! And ate it beside me like "I'm sorry! I'm so hungry!"

17 things not to do when your partner is pregnant

tinybranches: slept for most of my 17 hour labor even when I was yelling "wake up! They're breaking my water" and he was like "so?" I could have murdered him. He also left multiple times to eat food. Ugh. Still pissed.

Oh and then he kept going home after delivery to sleep and wouldn't get to the hospital til like 3 or 4 and he asked for a paternity test when he signed the birth certificate!:(

my mom and sister both acted like jerks too they got in a fight with me because I wouldn't let them change a diaper. I was a new mom for heaven sakes! I wanted to do everything and make sure everything was right. They screamed at me and ruined my trip and the nursesat in there with me while I cried for hours

consciousmommy: Nap while I chased around our 1 year old

sophdodson: needing a sleep in the middle of a 16.5hr labour because HE was tired

vickibrun: Told me my face looked puffy when I was eight months pregnant (it really didn't need pointing out!)

fkschultz22: Felicia from Georgia – The delivery room had a TV so my husband had to go get his playstation so he could watch Netflix and play Madden while I was being induced

sylvie7754: Going hunting and shutting of his phone, we agreed he could go if he checked his phone often. I went into labor 3 weeks early and had to send a family friend into the bush to search for him. He just made it to the hospital in time!

17 things not to do when your partner is pregnant

Babyledeverything: Rabeia from Chicago, Illinois. Not exactly during pregnancy but right when my little boy was born, he called his family back home to give the good news. The word spread superfast among family members and within next 10 mins he started receiving congratulations calls on Skype, facetime and other apps that use video calling. He totally forgot about me and for the next four to five hours, all he cared about was showing off the baby. Note that during this period, I had severe haemorrhage (dangerous bleeding like a fountain of blood) and still all he cared at that timewas showing the baby in the nursery to family overseas on skype. And it wasn't like this was our first baby, he was our fourth child and second boy :(

heartsoxo25: Hello…LOL mine too never wants water but the moment I get a glass we end up sharing it just so he doesn't get up

I'm 33 weeks pregnant n not only is he not helpful but he now wants me to crack his back by standing on him… since I weigh more than him now (165)

ladymac83: He's 6'4 so putting things away on top of shelves…oh, and not going to the bathroom in my place. He should've found a way to pee in the middle of the night on my behalf

jennagal33: Mine would be us having to stop for gas on the way to the hospital while I was having strong contractions when I had been reminding him over and over to be sure the car had gas in it for when I went in to labor. If there are any guys reading this, make sure you have gas in the car at all times! Don't wait until tomorrow to fill it up!!!

__just__us__: Haha taking selfies in the delivery room as I was having contractions screaming my brains out lol…he was entertaining tho lol love him

17 things not to do when your partner is pregnant

angelam1982: When I was completely off my food I was hamstering little snacks to eat and when I finally felt I could eat something I'd go to the cupboard and find it gone. I never had the energy to get dressed and go to the shop again. He was amazing though as usually making sure I had things in whilst he was away at work and doing all the house work so I didn't have to worry about it and make myself ill trying

kdcollier: I got sent straight from my dr apt to the hospital. I didn't have my bags packed but had been putting the things I wanted packed into the laundry basket. When I called my husband to tell him to head to the hospital, I told him to grab the laundry basket. He brought the basket full of dirty clothes from our closet instead

pumpydavies: The least helpful thing my hubs did was to accidentally turn his mobile to "do not disturb" mode in the middle of the night when they had to break my waters and prepare for an emergency csection!!! I wasn't impressed when the nurse quietly asked me did I have an alternative number for my husband as he wasn't answering!!! Arghhhh I could've killed him when he finally got to the hospital an hr or so later (Sara from Wales)

udderaccess: 1st baby: refused to so a practice run to hospital then didn't know where to go, pulled up and locked me in the car to go in and find out. 2nd baby he refused to listen to me that we wouldn't make it to the hospital, got a few blocks from the house and had to pull over to "catch"

Knowing
Your Limits

Although there were no gunshots,
War had definitely been declared.

I can't say that I enjoyed writing this chapter. Like most men I don't like to admit I that I have limits, either physical or mental. However, anyone who's ever had me on their team at a pub quiz would probably say I was of no immediate use in the mental stakes. They would go on to tell you that I am best left to fetch drinks at the bar, or high five the smarter members of the team. As much as I loved being involved with all aspects of baby-raising, I look back on a few memories and realise that perhaps I let my enthusiasm get the better of me, and took on a little too much at times.

You see since Lilly-Jo was born well over three years ago, I've pretty much done every bath and every bedtime. I felt it was the best chance I was ever going to have to build connection, seeing that I work all day and only see her for maybe one or two hours a night. This routine also gave Louise a chance to zone out for a while and recharge. I can say that my tenure of sleep instructor started off pretty well. Little babies tend to do quite a lot of sleeping, especially when they start to get into a routine. So, apart from some wild nights during teething, I was able to get Lilly-Jo off to sleep fairly painlessly during those first months. And believe me, there is no greater satisfaction than being able to successfully get a child to sleep. Relatives gasp; wives look on with admiration, and strange stroller-pushing folk stop you in the street to offer vast sums of money for the secret key to unlock the gates of nod.

OK. OK. So the last one isn't really true but I'm sure on occasion some parent I didn't know looked down at my slumber-ridden child and dared to dream that dream. As with everything though, you never have to wait too long before you are thrown a curve ball. For me that ball came swift and suddenly, without prior announcement and with little time to pull back and make a new sleep plan. Did you guess that this came right around the time she turned one?

You see our little lady moved very quickly out of the afternoon nap stage and straight into the "let's stay awake for a twelve hour stretch" stage. Here she was able to stay up from 7am till 7pm but unfortunately she was absolutely shattered by the end of it. There is no explaining the chaos, anarchy and unpredictability of a tired toddler to anyone other than another parent who has one of these sleep deprived little people. These kids summon a force of energy from the bottom of the earth just to cry about being tired; the sound will ricochet straight down your vertebrae. The other side of this newfound ability to resist naps was that at least three times a week she would falter and crash out during the day, sometimes for much longer than she would have normally.

There were days when I knew that I could be potentially up till 11pm just trying to get her to sleep. A nap, or lack of a nap, combined with her resistance to sleep, could unleash a kind of hell in the nursery that was heard all around the neighbourhood. She would scream and have a fit for hours whilst simultaneously trying to clamber out of her cot to get downstairs and play. All the while I would be trying to gently coax her leg back over the rail and tempt her with stories or pacifiers.

She would cry herself to sleep while standing up before finally dropping off, shortly before I passed out myself from exhaustion. These were the dark days my friends.

Although I look back on that time now and laugh I realise it did fill me with dread for the few months that it lasted. Sometimes I'd have to collect myself at the front door when I knew it had been a nap day. What a trooper Louise was during those days. She often offered to do those bed times even though she was shattered but I very rarely took her up on it. Looking back, I wish now that I had done so. No one wants to admit there are days when you don't look forward to coming home knowing what's going to happen. You must admit it when it begins to happen because it will happen and you should know it's perfectly OK to think it and admit it. Sometimes, it's the only way you'll find a bit of sanity!

Remember, this book is reality, so don't be too shocked to hear there were things I didn't like. The flip-side is that I absolutely love doing diapers and baths, to a point where I get annoyed when I can't. So whatever you do, don't do what I did on occasion and try to soldier through the hard times without raising the white flag! Raise that flag when you need to and take a break. It's good for your mental health, and for your relationship with your partner and your kids. We can be stubborn, we men folk, but it's not good for you. If you've been considerate towards your partner then I'd be pretty certain the door will swing your way when it needs to. I do expect one day Louise and I will both get a rest...maybe even at the same time? Until that day, we both do our best to stay calm when the craziness comes to town.

Just as a side note, though, I still do bed time pretty much every night to this day, but with a lot less screaming now. I learned so much during those tough times that I can construct a peaceful bedtime no matter what the situation. On the difficult days though I try to remember this old saying: "what doesn't kill you only makes you tired".

The Fire

If you're not happy,
then no one else has a chance.

Despite having a very happy home life I recently had a few moments recently where I felt the balance in my life wasn't quite right. Sometimes the pressures of adult life, coupled with work and raising a family, clouds the way you think about yourself or blurs your perceptions of how you feel. It's almost always the case that new mums and dads put themselves second to their children and to each other. They disregard what they want for themselves in order to give what's needed to others. Louise and I are no different in this regard. Over the course of writing this book I unwittingly discovered a few things about myself; notably why at times I may not have been feeling as good within myself, as I should have. There is no question that the pressure of raising kids and providing for my new family can make things difficult sometimes.

What I know is that all parents feel it. It would have been pretty easy to single out the pressure as the reason I was lacking a little self-fulfilment. Or, I could have blamed the long hours I do at work as a factor. What I discovered was that neither of those things were the cause of my inner angst. In fact, I realised that the cause was because I'd become stuck in the past. I had become "that guy" who sits in a bar and thinks about all the (glorious) things they have done, rather than thinking about the things that were still ahead to do. It was as if those moments of years gone by were the best moments I was ever going to get to do for myself. It just seemed that there was no time left for my own pursuits anymore, nor was there even enough money left at the end of the week to pursue them. You don't really understand how family life takes its share of money earned and leaves little for personal indulgences. I don't think it's a selfish thing to want things and alone-times for yourself. I have found it's very hard to balance your wants and to put yourself before your family. It's common, and it's nothing to be ashamed about at all. We are human, after all, aren't we? Becoming a parent doesn't mean we suddenly lose all sense of self and self-indulgence, nor should we!

What I miss and longed for was the time I used to have for keeping up with my sporting interests. This just seemed to be getting harder and harder to do. I'd also been using that difficulty to give myself a reason not to do any of the things that I used to do that were such a big part of me. I put it out of my mind, and that in turn was making me feel ever more distant from my old self. I had, in a metaphysical sense, let the fire within me dwindle a bit. Those day trips or overnight adventures driving to the beach to surf were what I craved. It sounds pretty simplistic, but really, I've never been a terribly complicated person. It's always been easy to keep a smile on my face. The element of escape I was missing wasn't about getting away from the pressures of family life, it was about being alone, even if it was just for a few hours a week; alone to just be "me". Every man (or woman) who has a family, or who is single even, needs to have an individual pursuit that keeps boosting their zest for life.

It's unimportant what gives you that individual zest for life (unless it's illegal and entirely immoral). What's important is that you have something which does. It could be rock-climbing, fly-fishing, or playing chess. I certainly wouldn't describe surfing in the UK as living on the edge by any means, but it is what helps me to be me! Having the time for yourself, even if it isn't the amount you used to have, is vital for your inner happiness. The difficult thing for me to understand was that while I was getting plenty of satisfaction from my role as a dad, that satisfaction wasn't balanced out by the pleasure I was used to feeling as an individual. Self-satisfaction, or fulfilment as an adult, can come from many different sources. So don't box yourself in, and don't be afraid to go out and explore new things.

You have to know that I get huge satisfaction being a dad, and once your babies get a little older and you actually see them enact things you've taught them, there can be no happier moment to witness (unless it's a curse word they've heard you use). There's also plenty to be proud of in the job you do every day, and I enjoy being able to do something that provides for my family. Sure, I spend way too much time at it, but I was doing what I thought was the best I could do. Instead of continuing to accept all of that for what it was and continue on the path of self-neglect, I decided to change, and to stop making excuses for how I felt. I changed the hours I worked and I worked on my spending habits to take the pressure off money worries. I also decided to stop drinking because I felt that it had anchored me to the past and didn't fit in with the present.

I promised myself I'd do more for my own pursuits while continuing to devote as much time to my family as I always did, if not more. It's surprising how much better I felt by just deciding to better myself. Even if it doesn't work, at least I tried—and I think that's all you really can do. I can say that in the few months since I've adopted these changes I really have felt like a new person. Although I know I will always have to work hard and keep the balance, I definitely feel more positive as a whole. Throughout this, I've also become acutely aware now of how it must feel for Louise to be a stay-at-home mum in a way that I never understood before.

"Millennia" mums have more often than not been the mums who have stayed at home and sacrificed their own dreams to care for the family. Sometimes they might only do it for a few short years or sometimes they do it for much longer. I want to continue to be aware of what Louise wants to try to do after the kids are a little older, when they won't need her 24/7, as they do now. I don't want there to be a revelation one day when she realises suddenly that the babies are grown up and she hadn't made plans for herself and own pursuits. I know mums never want to be reminded that their babies are going to grow up but sadly, babies do grow up. I hope she appreciates one day that I encouraged her to look a bit into the future for herself. I'd encourage you all to do the same for your loved one.

So perhaps it's a little presumptuous of me to be writing a book like this. Maybe I didn't have it together enough, although at least I could admit that. The last four years have been an immense amount of fun raising my kids, and I put a huge amount of effort into both tasks. It wasn't always easy, but you forget about those times pretty quickly and I'm only left with the good memories.

This is something I've learned in my journey so far as a new dad. I'm not expecting that it will necessarily relate perfectly to anyone else, but nothing ever does from father to father.

When it comes to the happiness of the members of your family, it's not the happiness of your partner that's most important, nor is it that of your kids. It's actually your happiness that matters. You're not any good to anyone if you're not content within yourself—or at least striving to be, if you're not. If you're not happy then you can't really make other people happy. How will you experience or inspire joy for your family if you can't feel it for yourself?

It's those safety announcements on planes that tell you to first fix your own oxygen mask before helping others. I never quite understood that until now, but it's a no-brainer. It's harder to help someone else if you are struggling for breath yourself. The context in that definitely applies to parenting as well.

Never stop striving for your own goals. It will make your role as a dad so much more fulfilling, and that's what the fire within is really all about. Just remember you don't have to be perfect to be a great dad. You just have to be happy being one.

The Trap

Repeat after me:
'You cannot babysit your own kids!'

There is no question that the role you'll play in your family's life is different now, compared to what it might have been a few generations ago. The person responsible for taking care of the children has changed gradually throughout the years. I don't think anyone would argue that, in the past, the task of raising children on a day-to-day basis was largely left to the women of the family. These days I often read about and see real examples of just how much men are more involved in the raising of their kids. Our dads, and the dads of generations since passed, would never have been as involved as today's dads are. I believe a lot of this is due to the fact that as there is so much more equality in the work place, women are working just as much as men.

Long gone are the days you might see in TV shows like *Madmen*. In a throwback to the 1950s, a suited-husband strolls through the front door from work and is greeted with a martini. He then sits down, puts his feet up on a comfortable footrest and reads the newspaper, while the dutiful wife cooks the dinner. The kids play quietly around him. While I'm sure this may happen now and then,

in some parallel universe, I don't think it's very common these days. I'm almost certain that your wives don't greet you with a martini and a newspaper...or do they? Don't tell me, please. And really, have you ever known kids to play quietly around someone who is trying to relax with their feet up? All I can tell you is that if you can't hear anything from my kids, they are most definitely up to something they're not supposed to be doing.

If you don't find men taking charge a lot within the household, I can say that I do see men really take charge of perhaps the less exciting tasks, especially at social events or outings. Let me give you an example; babies and weddings. If you take a baby to a wedding, I can guarantee that at a really inopportune moment, your baby will start screaming, uncontrollably. These moments include:

1. Just as the couple is about to say 'I do',
2. The best man is just about to give that speech you've been waiting for two years to hear.

I've seen it many times and more often than not, it's the dad who takes the child outside to console them or change their diaper. I have noticed wives being given compliments on their husband's efforts, and I have been indirectly complimented via my wife as well. The person giving the compliment is typically of the older generation and will say something along the lines of...'Aren't you lucky to have a husband like that?' While it's nice to have your efforts acknowledged, don't fall into a trap of believing that you're doing something out of the ordinary. You're really only doing something that you should be; helping when needed.

With my case in point, I don't think Louise is particularly lucky to have me as a very *hands-on* dad. When we decided to have children it was always discussed and known that ours would be a very equal partnership. She is no more or less lucky to have me than I am to have her. Until I see people applauding her for changing a diaper, I'm quite happy to avoid being singled out for any heroic actions. I also think that the description babysitting should never be used when it comes time for a man to stay home and mind his kids while his partner goes out. Again, while you often hear others—and even dads themselves using that term, I don't think it's really possible for you to babysit your own kids.

For example, in the whole history of the world I don't think there has ever been a case of a woman saying, 'Oh I'm sorry I can't go out tonight, I'm babysitting my kids'. It sounds weird even to say it. So I think more than anything the "hero trap" is a state of mind that we can fall into when it comes to looking at our roles as dads. It might be more accurately described as seeing yourself in a secondary role to your partner's role as the prime caregiver. Even though my wife does stay at home and gives the majority of care, my opinion and assistance is only a phone call away. When I arrive home I take on the main role as much as possible.

I do believe, in our defence, that there is probably meant to be a difference in the roles that a mum and dad have in raising children. You need to look at it in an evolutionary sense. Louise has that nurturing maternal instinct that I'm afraid to say I don't have. Even though I love them just as much as she does, I certainly don't experience the emotions of my children to the acute level that she will. I also know that they will almost always ask for their mother when they are sick or have injured themselves (usually after playing with me). It seems that babies and young children are programmed to want their mum in times of crisis and I have talked about that in greater detail in another chapter. I've never tried to duplicate Louise's role; it's different to mine and is equally defined in what I do and cannot do, as well as in a more biological sense.

At times we can also fall into the trap of thinking that a woman is somehow programmed to know exactly what to do with children, especially when they are newborn. I have to admit I did sort of convince myself, in a few days of madness after Lilly-Jo was born, that of course she would know how to take care of her. Truth is though, that she had no more clue than I did. I think if you're going to be of any use to your partner early on, you should never buy into this misconception. Also, don't ever confuse maternal instinct with knowledge. Your partner will have an amazing instant bond with your baby that has probably been developing slowly ever since she discovered she was pregnant. This doesn't necessarily mean that she will all of a sudden have encyclopaedic knowledge of all things baby, after the birth; or all of a sudden magically know how to breastfeed, or any other task that's new to her.

I remember when Lilly-Jo was very young we were having massive issues with the formula she was having after Louise had to stop breastfeeding due to ill health. Something was causing her acute diarrhoea and many, many sleepless nights. We didn't know at the time that it was the formula itself causing her issues, because she was also eating solid food. It turned out she had a temporary intolerance to lactose, which eased once we removed that formula type. I was also able to find someone who could recommend a diet for Lilly-Jo that would help her to heal after that little trauma.

I know I'm probably getting off on a health tangent here but that is what a lot of what this chapter is about. When it comes to any big decisions, or trying to find a resolution to issues affecting your little one's health, you need to be making yourself heard. Don't fall into the trap of taking a backward step and leaving the weight of the decisions down to your partner.

So speak up if you think you have something useful to say, even if it's seemingly in opposition to what she thinks. Two heads are better than one, and as long as you're not critical of her, I'd hope she would be grateful that you're trying to offer insight into your baby's wellbeing. I can't say I ever came up with too many ideas that solved any medical crisis with our little ones, but I was always good at researching any issues we were having. Finding people to help you is sometimes half the battle when it comes to solving issues with poorly little ones. So again, don't expect she will know what to do, and that she will just take them to the doctor and everything will be alright.

The wellbeing of your baby will be first and foremost on her mind more often than you, and it can wear her down mentally. Make sure you shoulder some of that burden for her, and I promise you that the more you do it, the more your confidence will grow, and the more she will value your opinion in tough situations.

Dads In
The Kitchen

If you eat broccoli, they'll eat broccoli (eventually).

Years ago, there weren't many books around for us *wannabe, New Age* dads. We are now, however, living in an age when men have moved into, and taken over family kitchens at such a rapid rate that it's fast becoming the norm.

I've been cooking since I was quite young, and always enjoyed it. Cooking is something that I love to also encourage other new dads to do for their families, especially their little ones. You see, one of the most exciting times for me in relation to love of food and cooking, was when Lilly-Jo turned six months old and was ready to start eating solid foods. This is generally the average age that babies start to be weaned, the world over. I remember the first time my daughter tried food; it was Xmas day, 2012. We decided that apple would be the first food that she would taste so I steamed and mashed some fresh juicy apples the night before. We all gathered around her high chair in the morning, excitedly expecting to see all manner of chewing and swallowing. Instead, she took one mouthful of that apple, so lovingly prepared by her dad, and promptly spat it back out. This routine continued for a few days but of course she eventually got the hang of it, and then she really seemed to enjoy what I was making her.

It's very fulfilling being the provider of your baby's food and I understand how a mum who usually does all the feeding, must find it very satisfying. This chapter will talk about the best ways to start your little ones down the path to healthy eating. I also want to really encourage all of you new dads out there to take a leading role in feeding your little ones too; time spent cooking and sharing a meal around the table together through the years is really rewarding. And think about this…Imagine the satisfaction of your wife announcing to family and friends that daddy is taking care of Baby's culinary needs! I know my wife, Louise, enjoyed having one less thing to worry about.

There is no golden rule at what age you start your baby eating solid foods, but it's a good idea to follow their cues. If they are able to hold their head and trunk upright (if not actually sit without support), then it may be time to introduce food. Similarly, if they are showing a keen interest in your food then that could be a sign that it's time to get yourself in the kitchen. Generally speaking though, the most advisable age to start solids is around six months of age. Some people do start sooner but it's always a good idea to consult your family doctor if you are unsure.

When it comes to different ways of introducing your baby to foods there are two main approaches you can take. Firstly there is the traditional way of steaming and mashing fruits and vegetables into purées and spoon-feeding baby. The other method you can follow is called "baby-led weaning" which is essentially starting your baby directly onto soft finger foods. This method, as the name suggests, is all about letting your baby set the pace and graze and explore the feel of foods at their leisure.

There is no right or wrong choice as every baby is different and some take better to one method or the other. I will discuss both feeding approaches further on so you can get a better idea of what's involved. Whatever method you decide to try, just remember this golden rule: "Food before 1 is just for fun". This golden rule is very helpful and reminds us that up until the age of 12 months, babies generally get enough nutrition from their milk feeds, so the process of weaning them onto solids is not critical to their survival.

So relax a bit, the weaning process should be enjoyable—and even fun for both parents and babe. It's also important that you let your Health Practitioner know of any feeding concerns, concerns about food allergies, or even concerns about when to start your baby on solids. Your family doctor will have all the information you need.

MAKING HOMEMADE BABY FOOD

Whenever I'm talking to someone who is undecided about whether or not to feed their baby homemade food or commercial food from a jar, I simply ask them to try both and see which one they would prefer. You can never really replace the taste of fresh food.

The process of making baby food is pretty simple and I found it very enjoyable, even if it was 1am when I finished on some nights. There is a wealth of books out there on how to prepare your baby's food. Books by authors such as Annabel Karmel and Ruth Yaron spring to mind, and I highly recommend their books to help get you started. Essentially, what's involved is selecting various fruit and vegetables; steaming, baking or roasting them and then turning them into a purée using a blender or a food processor, stick mixer or even a masher. It does take time to do all this but once I got into a groove it was pretty painless. I generally allocated one night a week (*and a few beers*) to it so that I was always ahead of the game and had a good supply stashed in the freezer. If you're going to choose this method you should still allow baby to handle and taste the foods— whether that's by letting them handle the spoon or by giving them something to gnaw on like a steamed carrot stick. This way, baby can enjoy food with all of the senses, and it makes it more fun too.

HOW TO MAKE HOMEMADE BABYFOOD APPLE PUREE

1 Select 4-6 juicy organic apples.

2. Peel and slice into medium pieces, being careful to remove all the seeds.

3. Add 2-3 inches of water to your steaming pan and steam apples until just tender.
Remember to cook a few apple pieces in the water below to create a stock which can be used in the next step.

4. Place the steamed apples in a food processor and blend until smooth . You can use your water from step 3 to make a nice consistency if necessary, or use plain water. I prefer to use the cooking water as plain water only dilutes the flavour; a bit like pouring water instead of gravy on your Sunday roast!

5. Carefully spoon mixture into freezer trays. Baby will only eat very small amounts early on so it's best to freeze in 1oz portions .

6. Once tray is full, cover with a lid or aluminium foil. This will stop contaminates getting in to the food during freezing. Also, write the name and date on the lid. This helps if you're prepping more than one type of food at a time. Apples, pears and melons all look identical once frozen.

7. When the food is thoroughly frozen, carefully remove and place in a zip lock freezer bag and squeeze out the air before sealing. Remember to label with the name and the date; use within 4-6 weeks.

8. To defrost, place foods in a covered dish and leave overnight in the refrigerator. To warm, microwave in a microwave-safe container or use a Lillypot pan.
Always be careful to ensure food is the correct temperature before serving to baby. Bon appetite!

APPLE
27·8·15

APPLE

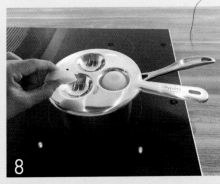

Need help?
@Babyfooduniverse
Instagram

Playing with food is important in establishing a healthy relation-ship with foods and eating.

When making your own baby food it is advisable to make large batches and freeze them. This is what I did for Lilly-Jo's homemade baby foods. All that Louise (my lovely wife) had to do was select what she wanted and simply defrost and serve. She loved how easy I had made it for her and once she settled into a routine and knew what the baby bird liked, it was plain (albeit messy) sailing. With this method of baby feeding you can really make your partner's life so much easier and you'll be the toast of the play dates too—which isn't so bad—is it?

Need help?
wholesomebabyfoodguide.com

BABY-LED WEANING

Having run a baby-related business for a few years now I see firsthand how popular this method has become with parents. Essentially BLW replaces puréed food with finger food right from the start and lets babies feed themselves at their own pace from the age of six months. It's generally advisable to start after six months of age as before then the vast majority of babies simply don't have the motor skills to be able to feed themselves.

During the early stages of baby-led weaning, parents usually try baby with sticks of steamed fruit and veg that they are able to easily hold in their hand. Primarily baby is sat in their highchair, and with constant parental supervision is allowed to do whatever they wish with the food in front of them. Unfortunately, that doesn't always mean it entering their mouths, as they might find it much more interesting to rub it in their hair or simply stare at it. This is the reason why it's called "baby-led", as there is virtually no interference from the parent, and baby decides when he or she is ready to eat. Again, with this method there are a wealth of books available on the topic. Authors like Gill Rapley and Tracey Murkett spring to mind, if you're interested in learning more about this approach.

While we mostly started Lilly-Jo on purees with some finger foods we decided we would do the opposite with Huey. He was a much more "grabby" baby and is obsessed by food when he sees it. So while we have still used some purées, we used BLW more with him, and found it suited him very well.

People like to describe this method as "baby eating what you eat". For the most part, this is very true. After the initial stage of getting baby started with simple sticks of steamed food you can essentially feed them anything that you're eating! Just remember not to add the salt until you've served their portion. When I say anything, I really mean it. I mean I've seen pictures of eight month old babies gnawing on lamb chops! Seriously!

Although I've not really elaborated on the variety and types of food that parents feed their kids, in each of these methods there are some amazing recipes out there in the virtual world, free of charge. Once you've decided on your approach it's so very easy to start following a Facebook or Instagram account dedicated to that approach of feeding. I've always found the folks who run them eager to help and hand out advice. Simply search #homemadebabyfood or #BLW and you'll be bombarded with choices and ideas.

I also wanted to touch on the best time to feed baby in the early days. Generally, babies starting solids are more receptive to foods

Baby-Led Weaning

Babies of six months want to explore food. They need a variety of textures and tastes, in sticks and chunks that they can grab with their whole hand. They may not eat a lot (or even anything) at first - but they will be learning so much!

By about one year, most babies are enjoying eating familiar foods and trying new ones. They can manage smaller pieces with their fingers and may be beginning to use cutlery.

earlier in the day when they are less tired and when they already have had a milk feed first. Remember they are new to this so it's best to have them in a happy, receptive state before you start. You'll have plenty of time to learn their feeding patterns later, so for the early part treat their first tastes as a dessert—not a main meal.

Need help?
rapleyweaning.com

THE CONCLUSION

When it comes to choosing what type of approach to take it's important to be pretty flexible and watch for the cues from your baby. I know many parents who have tried different methods only to find it didn't really agree with them, or didn't suit their babies at the time. Some babies simply aren't interested in purées and would rather raid your plate. Similarly, some can have sensory issues and can become a bit overwhelmed with whole pieces of food so early. So don't get too disheartened if your chosen method doesn't quite go to plan; it's all about being flexible and doing what is right for Baby.

The best thing about either approach is that you're going to be giving them fresh, wholesome food, and that's more important than which method you choose. I do personally however try not to get too worked up about every single thing they are eating and whether it's organic or not. I mean our house is on one of the busiest roads in London and is directly under the flight path for Heathrow airport, so typically the air they are breathing isn't that fantastic, and if a few not-so-organic bits and pieces get onto their plate, I'm sure there are greater worries in life.

Probably the most important thing to remember though, more than anything, is to constantly supervise your babies when they are eating. Choking is a major hazard, and should never be taken lightly. If you're on your own while feeding them there are no bathroom breaks or TV watching. Babies often don't make much sound when choking, so, if you're engrossed in Facebook or something you may not hear them. Might be worth a mention, while we are talking about choking, is to go ahead and do a first aid course for babies. It typically only takes a few hours and is readily available in most urban areas. There are very specific ways to deal with a choking infant so if you're reading this, or have a baby on the way and haven't done one; get off your butt and book one now.

Apart from the thought of choking, weaning is a fabulously fun time. And it's so important to make the most of it because it comes and goes so fast. You can set your child up for a lifetime of healthy eating just by what you do in the first few years of life. Babies also learn by example though, so try to practise what you preach. You can always lock yourself in your room if you really need that glazed doughnut—your children will have plenty of time once they are older to buy their own doughnuts.

But a good weaning experience, and the feeding years that follow will be one of the most important things you ever do for your child, so be the dad that realises that early on.

Need help?
superhealthykids.com

First Friends

I really thought we'd be friends forever, Adam.

I remember one of the first friends I ever had, very clearly. His name was Adam and he lived just down the road from us. We were both around seven at the time. Although we went to the same school, we were in different classes, so our friendship—from what I remember, only really came into play on weekends. The thing about early friendships is that they seem to last forever when you're a little kid. In reality, these friendships may have only existed for a few weeks or just over a summer. We were "tight" from what I remember and used to do a lot of bike riding around our small town. Parents could let their kids do that back in those days. Things were safe and we never had any trouble.

I don't remember how it happened, but right in the middle of that friendship he moved away. Strangely, about a year later, he returned to the school one day to say hello to everyone and to see his old friends. I can only assume his parents brought him, although they were nowhere to be seen. One of the more senior teachers was showing him around all the different classes; it was like he was some long lost golden child. Even at that time, the showcasing seemed a little out of proportion for an eight year old. Looking back on it, it may have been that his parents had some kind of social standing I was unaware of, which added to the unusual pedestalling. I remember it very clearly when Mrs Harris brought him into my class and announced his arrival. I was standing at the back of a huddled group and I figured I'd wait till everyone had finished fawning so we could catch up.

Instead of him taking the time to come and talk to me, he completely blanked me out; not even a glance in my direction. He left the room without as much as one word. Yes, I'm still a bit gutted about the whole affair even thirty odd years later. Some things are never really understood when you're young and tend to leave profound impressions upon you. That story might not be interesting to you but it just so happens that right at this moment in time, Lilly-Jo is acquiring her first real friends outside the realms of our family circle. She has so far had a number of different play dates and they are going well. The other girls seem very nice and possess just enough "crazy" that they make a perfect match for our little lady. Like any play date with young children, disaster is always on the brink and can bubble over at any moment. Anyone who's had a three year old will know exactly what I'm talking about—the odd fight over a toy and subsequent sulking, then re-bonding over a chocolate biscuit; becoming best friends again as if nothing ever happened.

Play dates are an excellent way to gauge how well you're doing at parenting, at least on average anyway. It can go either way though, I'm afraid, and just because you think the kids have learned to share doesn't always mean it will be put into practice. Don't worry if it goes wrong. You're not alone. Hundreds of parents have their heads buried in their hands while sitting in a house they've never been in before, watching that successful play date go pear-shaped.

It's immensely important to me that Lilly-Jo and Huey learn how to make friends. For most dads who work, there aren't too many opportunities to encourage friendships. I only have Lilly-Jo in social situations a few times a week. As much as I enjoy taking her to the play centre and being her playmate on Sundays, I'm always encouraging her to meet other kids. Some days she is more receptive than others so I just roll with it. Parents forget that some days, kids can be just like them and not be bothered with stuff from one day to the next. When I was watching Lilly-Jo and one of her friends play recently, it really reminded me of all those friendships I had when I was very young. I'm lucky in a way because my best friend now, was my best friend way back before I turned ten. Along the way I had many short-term friends and there is value in those friendships too. As I said earlier, these fleeting friendships seemed like they'd last forever but more likely than not, they just fizzled out.

When you're little, very simple things can alter friendships and many times these are out of your control. For example, changing class at the start of a new school year, or even moving to a house a few blocks away can vastly alter who your friends are. I mean, in high school I'd have been gutted to have lost all my hard-earned friends but little people seem to be able to adapt to all that. I imagine their minds are set very much in the present in terms of who they know, and what's right in front of them at the time.

It makes me wonder what the future holds for Lilly-Jo and her new "besties". They only live two blocks away from each other and I expect they will remain there for the next ten years or so. Although I'm fairly sure they won't go to the same school, I wonder if they'll always know each other. Sometimes when I'm back in Tasmania I walk down the street past someone I used to spend large amounts of time with thirty five years ago. We pass each other as if we are complete strangers, but I wonder if that's just because we don't know what to say to each other. Maybe the girls will be the same when they grow up? Only time will tell, but it would be nice to think they will always be connected, even if in the future it's just by way of a friendly hello in one of the local pubs. If not, I guess she will always have this book and we can remind her who her first best friends were.

One of the best things about being a parent is that you get to see with your own eyes what growing up is like. It's almost like watching a movie of your own early years. It's made me appreciate things more now that I see just how fleeting moments in time can be for my little ones. It's worth stopping to think about that every once in a while.

Incidentally, if anyone remembers a kid called Adam from Wynyard Primary School in Tasmania, Australia, circa 1982-1983, please get in touch and let me know. He may have been in Mrs Harris' class. He had blonde hair, rode a yellow bike and lived in Hales Street in a brick house. While I'm sure I'll survive if this affair doesn't get the closure it deserves, one thing is evidently clear; as you get older it becomes more and more important for you to still know some of the people who knew you when you were young.

I'm lucky to still have some very amazing friends from when I was young, and I really hope that I can teach and encourage Lilly-Jo and Huey to have those same connections. People you might not see for ten years but can instantly click back in without an utterance of small talk. Those are the kind of friendships I want for my kids.

Holiday Horror

It's a vacation, Jim, but not as we know it.

If I sit very still and squint with intense concentration I can just about remember what a holiday before children was like. Those hazy golden memories of mid-morning sleep-ins, sandy beaches and intervals of afternoon drinking with not a single repercussion in sight, wow!

The last time we ventured on a holiday (vacation) alone was when we went on our honeymoon way back in 2011. It was a lovely journey to Mexico. Alas that was to be our last as a single couple because baby Lilly-Jo just couldn't wait to join us. I'm not saying it was a lightning fast conception but let's just say if we named her after where she was conceived then she'd be called Hotel Transit Rodwell. It should have been a sign when Louise started feeling giddy after just ten days and we went in search of a pregnancy test. With much trepidation and a fair amount of descriptive charades we were able to get our hands on *Choppo*! Later I will touch on the perils of navigating pharmacies and medications abroad with kids.

Choppo, you see, was the brand name of the pregnancy kit we bought. Over the course of the remainder of the honeymoon and many, many more Choppos, those little pink lines grew ever darker. So did the realisation that two would soon be three. When you're about to become a parent you never realise that the many things

CAUTION ✈
HOLIDAY MAY NOT
GO AS PLANNED

you took for granted will never ever be the same. Your life together will never be the same as it was when it was just the two of you. One thing that definitely changed for us, and I expect for most parents, was our annual family holiday. It's very hard to quantify to single people exactly how difficult the first few times away are with a new baby.

So many things have to be considered that it feels at times like a military exercise, with a small screaming infant controlling the whole saga. The luggage that infants require is shocking enough on its own, let alone other hardware such as strollers or car seats that you'll need. I'm actually sometimes surprised they don't have a baby- passenger limit on planes, given the amount of excess baggage required. If I give you any advice about where to go on your first trip away, it would be to go somewhere you've already been before. At least then, when, and if something goes wrong, you won't feel so isolated, and you'll be able to easily navigate your way to help.

Our first trip was to Biarritz in France. We knew it well and that turned out to be very useful after how badly it went. About five days in, I was struck down with gastroenteritis of Herculean proportions. For two days I lay at the gates of hell. Louise passed me things with rubber gloves on, all the while scrubbing anything I went near. She used copious amounts of bleach, and we were praying that Lilly-Jo didn't fall victim to the super bug. It really wasn't the best time to be a man down. We were staying on the third floor and there were no lifts. Lilly-Jo was also just starting on solids so meal times with her were very full-on. Louise just had to carry on, as I was in no fit state to help anyone. Thankfully, two days later I awoke, back to normal, and desperate to get back to business. Unfortunately that very same morning Louise started to turn green...and we all knew what was coming!

Having been unable to surf and knowing I'd be a single parent for a few days, I sensed I had a very short window of opportunity. I grabbed my surfboard and bolted towards the beach. 'Try not to throw up just yet!' I shouted as I ran down the stairs. 'I'll be back in an hour.' I returned to the apartment 58 minutes later to be handed the baby. I watched as Louise descended into the hellhole I'd only just escaped. Even though it was a very unfortunate affair, I really enjoyed the challenge of the next few days being a solo dad. Lilly-Jo and I went to the beach; dined in the finest restaurants, and bonded over our love of baguettes as we patiently waited for Mummy to return to normal. I'd like to say our sickness record improved in the following years...but alas it was not to be!

There was also the vomiting bug in New York, and an attack from a feral cat in the Canary Islands which drew blood on Lilly-Jo's face; this required preventative treatment for infection. We have kind of gotten used to it now and our medical bag is always well stocked in preparation for anything ranging from grazed knees to Ebola. You see, finding medications you take for granted at home can sometimes be difficult abroad. You have the language barrier to deal with, and the worry of not being able to follow the instructions correctly. I have been in the position before of having to describe diarrhoea with a mixture of mime and sign language. It was a very low moment in my life that I wish not to visit again.

That's why it's crucial on our family holidays, to arrive at our destination fully prepared to survive the first 48 hours as if there were no shops open at all. Louise is very good at this, as are most mums. She makes sure that the babies have all their essentials packed into our luggage. Items such as diapers, formula and any medication we might need, as well as snack foods. Having enough of these things until you can find your bearings in a new place will make everything so much less stressful.

Moving away from the material side of holidays, the safety of my children is the biggest worry I face when abroad. In strange countries you just can't be complacent or take your eyes off them for a second. I was so petrified that someone was going to try and kidnap Lilly-Jo that I think I never really relaxed on our first vacation. I'm better now but I still have the fear—although once you learn to control it, trips away become more relaxed, normal affairs.

In saying that though, if there ever becomes an easy non-invasive way to microchip your child, I'd seriously consider it; I'm being half-serious when I say that. I do hope that I haven't put you off taking family holidays forever.

Holidays away can be stressful, but it is exciting showing kids different parts of the world, even if they can leave you pretty drained as a new parent. Sometimes it's just hard to unwind with little ones because they very rarely give you any time to yourself. When we are away we always take turns with the childcare and let the other go off for a few hours every other day to do something nice by themselves. For me this is surfing, and for Louise, it is exploring the towns or local markets. Don't fall into the trap of thinking you need to be a family unit a hundred percent of the time because you don't. Those hours you get to spend by yourself, while your partner looks after the kids, make for much better trips. We swear by it and it's sort of an unwritten rule that we follow to keep the two of us refreshed when we are away. Happy Travels to You.

You'll need these

Lost And Found

*The day my own mum lost me
in the shopping mall.*

I'll never forget the day my own mother lost me in a shopping centre. Actually, that's a lie because I was probably too young to remember being lost. The story has been told so many times that I can't decide if I remember what happened, or if I'm just imagining that I remember.

It happened in a busy shopping centre way back in the 70s in suburban Melbourne, Australia where I was born. Now, my mum is a fairly observant person and there were no mobile phones as a distraction back then, but as the old saying goes, she only turned her back for a second and Poof! I was gone. I'm not exactly sure how long I was missing but the police found me waiting at a busy intersection. You see, even at three years of age, I knew the way home. They took me to a security guard, who then took me to his office in control central.

The funny part of the story is that he was trying to ascertain what my name was and also what my mum's name was. So when he asked me my name, I replied, 'Tam'. When he asked what my mum's name was, I correctly replied, 'Pam'. Mum tells me that the poor confused security guard was sure that our names couldn't possibly be true. Needless to say, he put an announcement over the shopping centre's loudspeaker system, and a rather frantic mother came to collect her golden child.

I wanted to start this chapter with this story because this chapter is about lost children, literally and figuratively. There have been times that I've been with Lilly-Jo and have seen other kids who appear to be lost. When it comes to the supervision of little ones, I've witnessed some fairly different parenting approaches compared to mine. What you understand very quickly when you start taking your little ones to "uncontrolled" social play areas is that parenting styles vary greatly across society. I take Lilly-Jo to a variety of different play areas across west London and the vast majority of parents are really observant. On occasion, incidents happen with other kids when there is apparently no one watching them. There have been quite a few times that I've had to rescue a distraught kid who's found himself in a position on a climbing frame that he couldn't get himself out of.

I feel uncomfortable picking up strangers' kids, but when no one is watching them and they are upset, you don't have much choice. I also don't like to let Lilly-Jo see kids crying needlessly. There are unusual times when I'll be quietly reading her a story in the corner and another child will just snuggle up beside me and join in. I'm always happy to read to any kid who enjoys listening, but after thirty minutes have passed and no one has even noticed, it makes me a bit uncomfortable. Maybe I'm just a bit too overprotective? I just can't seem to relax in a play area if I don't have at least one eye on Lilly-Jo at all times. That's not to say I shadow and helicopter over her all the time. I try to give her space when she decides to make friends. I always take a step back and let her socialise, but you can be sure that I am always watching her intently.

In soft play areas, amongst others, there is so much colour and noise that it's really easy to misplace a kid. To make matters worse, many of these enclosed areas have more than one exit and with so many slides and tunnels in them, it's difficult to keep track of them. I suggest that before you let your kid loose in one that you give it a quick survey and find out if there is more than one way out. It can be very draining mentally when it comes to day trips alone with your little ones. It only takes a second for you to have your nose buried in your phone and for them to just slip away unnoticed. What won't go unnoticed by your partner is you turning up at your house without the child you left with! This is something I highly recommend not doing...not ever. I never thought about writing a chapter about keeping your child safe. I mean, your children are your children and it's not my business...but last week I witnessed an incident so shocking that it inspired this chapter.

I was in a family pub last weekend when I noticed a boy of about three, crying terribly. He was heading towards the door, which led straight to a narrow busy road, and the road does not have a sidewalk. Before I could get up, another woman had stopped him. Realising, obviously, that he was lost, she grabbed a member of staff and they went off to find the boy's parents. She returned a few minutes later looking particularly shocked so I leant over and asked her what had happened. She recounted that they found the boy's mother dining all the way at the back of the bar on the other side. It must have been a good fifty yards away. Apparently the woman hadn't even noticed he was gone and she offered no thanks for his safe return.

Slightly dumbfounded, the woman informed her that he was just about to walk out the door and the mother replied that she didn't care. I don't really know what to make of that entire story but I do find myself really feeling sorry for the little boy. Being lost is terrifying for kids.

I'm not sure if the rise of the Internet has made me more wary, considering all the abduction stories you hear about these days. Maybe they always happened and we just didn't know about it. I couldn't imagine the incredible guilt that would consume me if I lost one of my children due to my not being watchful. Even if it was only for a few minutes in a shopping centre, I always tap into that fear to remind me to be super-alert. It is hard not to be a little judgemental sometimes with other parents, especially with safety, and I apologise if I come across in a negative way. Perhaps I am indeed, too over-protective.

Only time will tell if that's been something I should have handled differently. I do hope you all keep your little ones safe, while still managing to give them their independence. If you succeed at this and stay sane, please write in and tell me how you did it.

Packing For The Apocalypse

Once you successfully pack a diaper bag,
they'll tell you who shot Kennedy.

I'd like to say that I remember where I went on my first solo public outing with a baby, but I don't. It's a big deal the day you first take your baby out alone and I was so focused on keeping her safe that I actually don't remember where it was we visited. It's safe to say that it was probably nowhere near train tracks or the local javelin throwing club. While I can't remember where Lilly-Jo and I went, I certainly do remember how I felt...scared...very, very, scared. I remember being so nervous the night before that I could barely sleep. I was lying there in the dark trying to imagine all the things that could go wrong on a visit to the proverbial duck pond, and preparing counter-terrorism plans in case something did. I mean ducks are fairly harmless, right? Certainly no duck could swim away with a baby...but, what if there was a gang of ducks? Perhaps they could over-power me and make off with our Lilly-Jo! I laugh now at what was going through my head all night...ducks...and misfired javelins.

It was sometime after Lilly-Jo was born that I actually got to take her out by myself. She spent a while getting herself into a good

DAY IN THE PARK!

 **+**  **=**

WHAT TO PACK;

2 x outfits
3 x nappies / diapers
Nappy cream
Toy
Bottles
Water
Changing mat
3 x Dummies / pacifiers
Wet wipes
Sunscreen
2 x bibs
2 x muslin cloths
Nappy sacks
Snacks

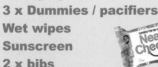

feeding routine so she was glued to her Mummy for a few weeks after the birth. By the time my chance had arrived for my first solo journey I had at least started to feel pretty comfortable with her. I believe that it's important before you go off on adventures that you feel at least mildly at ease with your child. There are subtle differences in cries, for example, and knowing the difference between a tired cry and a hungry cry make things easier to handle. Be warned though, there is also a cry called the "I'm not sure why I'm crying" cry. If this cry presents itself, you should attempt to feed, entertain and rock your baby to sleep, simultaneously. While I'm on feeding, make sure you know your child's mealtimes. These times very rarely change and the periods in between can be peppered with healthy snacks. It's important if your partner is the prime caregiver of your little one to really listen to what she says about meal times. Sometimes it can be the smallest things that send lunchtime into oblivion.

By the time your baby is a few months old there will be various tricks of the trade that only the prime caregiver will know. They have this saying in Australia—*she'll be right mate*—a casual reference implying things just work out OK, without much effort. All I can say is that if you don't listen to your partner on the subject of mealtime routine, she'll (most certainly not) be right! Don't be too proud or macho, because no one can know everything about their baby; suck it up and follow her advice when she speaks.

I think there are three key ingredients to having a successful outing with a baby:

- Planning
- Packing
- Positive attitude

There is also a variable fourth key point and that is to never, ever be hungover for these outings.

Now I'm not going to lie, as there have been many times in my life that I've enjoyed an alcoholic beverage. Unfortunately on a few occasions over the course of weekends, I have inflicted mild hangovers on myself that coincided with my having an energetic toddler for the day. I must tell you with brutal honestly that time, in fact, stood still on these days. I prayed to the lord of soft play centres that I be swallowed up into a giant hole in the carpet as punishment for my stupidity. You see, toddlers don't give a damn that you're tired. As lovely as they are, they display virtually no empathy for the first few years of life so don't expect any let-up.

I once read the Hollywood actor, Ryan Reynolds, describe blinking as a form of sleep when it comes to child-induced tiredness. I can recall many times the sheer joy of what an extended blink can feel like, so I'm fully on-board with his analogy.

Ironically this is, in fact, the last chapter I originally wrote of this book, and at the time it had been almost nine months since I had a drink. There are probably a few people who know me that after reading this will have just fallen off a chair or fainted, but I can assure you it's real. Don't worry though, I do intend to have a drink again but when, I can't say. Not drinking has been great for my weekend play dates with the kids. I have far more energy and patience than I normally would.

But, getting back to the first of the key ingredients of a successful outing—planning. It isn't so much about planning where you're going as it is about knowing what facilities are there when you arrive. Knowing if there are changing facilities or places to feed your little one are just as important as the actual activity you're going to be doing. There are excellent apps available on phones these days that tell you all sorts of things like this, so make sure you download one before you set off. For me personally, the key to a successful outing is to keep it really simple. Let's face it, unless your two year old is a budding Einstein, the science museum is no more fun than a random passport photo booth. I say this because for about a year, that was Lilly-Jo's favourite hangout in our local shopping centre. I have spent many hours in that booth pressing the touch screen and playing hide and seek outside.

For her, fun is not a complicated issue. She merely wants me to be involved with what she is doing and if that's residing in a photo booth then that's what fun is. I can't emphasise enough how important the actual play is and how unimportant the location is. I also like to keep travel times short, and rarely spend more than 30 minutes on a bus or train to get there. I realise that's not as easy for dads living in more remote areas, but it's one of the things I like about living in a city like London.

Before I move on to the next key point of a successful outing, I have to say that when it comes to packing a diaper bag, my wife has taught me everything I know. A good diaper bag is absolutely essential for a seamless outing. Sure, it will have cupcakes or unicorns on it but you need to get past this immediately. The very good bags are so well designed with various pockets, that they enable you to organise more items that a normal bag just won't allow. There will be times when you need to find a pacifier in 2.5 seconds, or a pair of scissors to open a formula container. You need to be able reach into that bag like you're a surgeon, getting what you need with the minimum of fuss.

That said, there will always be times when things go wrong. Sometimes, no matter how many diapers you bring, you'll still run out. You wouldn't think a kid could go through five diapers and two outfits in the space of three hours, but believe me, it happens. The best times are when you're carrying your toddler and poop leaks all over you. This has happened to me about three times now and it never gets easier to bear. It's moments like these, or when stocks are depleted, that it helps to have a little bit of MacGyver in you. I once ran out of diapers so had to use my t shirt (not the one that got pooped on) plus a few random hair bands to fashion what was essentially a pee dam. It wasn't pretty, but it got us home on the bus—and that's all that matters.

So there you have it...a basic lesson on how to approach an outing with your little one. Soon they will be off, out with friends, so try not to miss the chance for a bit of one-on-one time. Just save the beer for when you get home and toast your solo parenting successes in the glow of your now rested partner.

MY
PROUDEST MOMENT
OF FATHERHOOD

Proudest Moments Of Fatherhood

*How wrecking furniture
can make you untouchable.*

Even after four years of being a dad, this is by far and away my favourite moment of fatherhood—and it actually came along by accident. I've learned that many of the best events of this journey have a tendency to come along when you least expect them to.

In my dreams, I suppose before Lilly-Jo and Huey were born, I always had this vision of myself standing on the sidelines, soaking up the many glorious events where my children would triumph. I would then have that feeling of satisfaction, knowing that they had achieved their full potential. Before I go any further though, let me just explain the photo. I guess at no point in my life was I ever a person who left much to chance, and when Lilly-Jo was first born, I devoted myself entirely to her. While I accept there is an element of chance with anything you do in life, I was a little reluctant to let the universe take the majority stake in how she was raised.

In the first two weeks I changed every single diaper! Louise still remembers the day clearly when I returned to work and she had absolutely no idea how to do it. To be fair though, she was involved in a very steep learning curve involving breastfeeding. Now changing diapers is nothing compared to those first few weeks of trying to feed a new born...and you will see what I mean for yourself soon enough.

We both had our roles and we both put a huge amount of effort into them. My devotion to diaper-changing never waned. It wasn't until Lilly-Jo was about six months old that Louise pointed something out to me that I had never noticed. I'd been stationed at the end of our changing table for so long that my belt buckle had scraped the paint off. There now also stands a substantial groove in the woodwork that my belt had worn out. Who would have thought diaper changing would lead to this? I'm proud of that scraped paint and battered woodwork; it's a proud badge of support that I was there for Louise and Lilly-Jo when it really mattered.

Usually, where there is damaged furniture, there are scolded husbands, but on this occasion and on this piece of furniture, there was none of that. I can remember feeling a mixture of pride, and also shock, at the sheer amount of time I must have spent pressed against that change table. Lilly-Jo and I had many weird and wonderful conversations on that change table and although I can't remember what they were all about, I can promise they would have made no sense to anyone listening in. In reality, I never really overly cooed or spoke baby talk to Lilly-Jo. I've always talked to her in a very adult way and I think this is partly the reason why she had such advanced speech at an early age.

I know for certain that many dads out there share a universal reluctance for diaper changing, but I would really encourage you to get involved in it as much as you can. It's an opportunity for a bonding occasion. Think about it as the daddy version of breastfeeding, without the sore nipples! So, don't look for, or wait for the "big" moments. Appreciate all of the smaller ones that come your way.

It may seem strange to you that my proudest moment of fatherhood so far, isn't actually something my kids did, but it's something I did for them. Just remember that these moments might not be the flashy ones that scream the loudest but more the subtle ones that you almost didn't notice. When I look back now at that scratched table I feel a great sense of achievement, and it's something that no one ever has the power to take away from me.

From the moment your baby is born, every second that you spend with them counts, and every interaction you have with them has some bearing on the person they will become.

The Blueberry Bandit

When life throws you fruit,
add a scoop of ice cream.

I remember back in Grade 4, a teacher named Mrs Ferencz gave us a challenge. The challenge was to see how many times we could fold a piece of paper across itself. She said that it wasn't possible to fold it any more than eight times. She also added that if you could in fact fold it more than eight times, then it would be so thick it would reach the moon! The whole "moon" concept thing kind of went over my head a bit at the time. You see Mrs Ferencz was, from memory, the special teacher that doubled as the part-time teacher for the gifted kids. I can't really remember how I ended up in one of her afternoon classes; maybe I'd gotten lost on my way to special physical education lessons to work on my ball-catching? Or perhaps as I suspect, the school staff were just giving the average kids a taste of what a gifted kid's class felt like. Regardless of the reason, I thought the paper folding analogy would be a good lead into this chapter because, well, I get it now. The lesson was meant to provoke thought and interest in learning about what was essentially an impossible task. It reminds me of the time I first became a parent and how little I really understood about the concept of parenting, compared to what I do now.

There are certain things they don't tell you about becoming a parent. Actually there are a lot of things they don't tell you. I imagine if I could find a piece of paper big enough to write down all the things I've learned as a parent, I'd be able to lay it out into space and walk to the moon. One of the biggest things I didn't expect was the worry. You, and especially your partner, will worry incessantly about your babies. Even when they are yet to be born there is always the constant fear of them not making it. During our first pregnancy I would always ask Louise if the baby had kicked that day. I would do it in a fun way though, to mask the fact that I was actually enquiring if the baby was still alive in there. Sometimes babies go whole days without moving and that is scary as hell let me tell you. I'd love to say that the fear ends once the baby is born, but the thing is that the fear doesn't end with the birth; that my friends is only the beginning!

You see, in the early days we would both constantly check to be sure that Lilly-Jo was still breathing while she slept. I went even further and mostly checked her pulse (lung movement didn't seem enough). We both did this at least once every half hour for the first year of her life, sometimes without telling each other. We were so effective that our poor girl was checked for signs of life every fifteen minutes for at least 365 days in a row. I'd like to say we offered Huey the same blanket coverage but it was unnecessary in his case. The kid hasn't ever slept three consecutive hours in his six months. He hasn't even slept more than five cumulative hours in a 24-hour period for that matter! So while we do check in on him regularly as he sleeps, it's not the same workload. Huey is his own life barometer. Getting back to the story though, I was trying to discuss blueberries? Ah yes that's right, blueberries.

When Lilly-Jo was little we used to call her the blueberry bandit! Actually we called her the mango monster as well, such was her love of those two fruits. Mum or dad would spend many mornings hunched over a sieve turning these little berries into fine syrup that we would mix in with her morning porridge. This one particular morning the weather was quite glorious so we decided to feed her alfresco in the backyard in her highchair. Lilly-Jo was around nine months old at the time and was really starting to be very aware of the world around her, this made Sunday excursions a very exciting time for us. I remember the morning with such clarity. After break-fast we sat some more in the garden and "chatted" together. I could hear the whirr of the hairdryer upstairs as Louise readied herself, and the birds chirped in the garden. Life was glorious. Just then Lilly-Jo looked up at the sky with mouth agog. To my absolute horror I saw on the roof of her mouth what looked like a large purple growth. Fear shot through my body like a bolt of lightning and I feverishly tried to get another look. Yes it was purple! Yes it was huge and let me tell you, it was hideous. I gently scraped at it with my finger but it didn't budge! I sat back down totally lifeless; I couldn't even hear Lilly-Jo babbling because everything had gone dead silent.

What was it? Oh surely not? Could it be a cancer? Was she going to die? OMG, what could I do? In a split second this is what I decided to do. It might sound crazy but thought for thought, this is what went through my head, before common sense and calm prevailed:

OK, right this is bad! She's really, really sick! That thing in her mouth looks very terminal to me. I mean she can't have long to live? Hours? Days? We should take her to the ER straight away? No wait, but what if she dies tomorrow—then our lasting mem-ory will be of this moment. OK right, I'm not going to tell my wife, we are just going to have one last glorious day together before she leaves us! I will tell her tomorrow morning and we can go straight to hospital...

Then, all of a sudden, I came to my senses. I rushed upstairs and called to Louise to come quickly. Sensing my fear she bolted, mid-blow dry. She turned and ran, so quickly, in fact that the hair-dryer kind of stayed suspended in mid-air for a moment, just like in a cartoon. She too looked in Lilly-Jo's mouth and turned a shade of white I'd not seen since I washed out fine china from IKEA the night before. Collecting herself, she too tried to give it a nudge but it wouldn't budge. Lilly-Jo was starting to get a little annoyed at this stage and was refusing to open her mouth. We got it open one more time and scraped at it with a plastic spoon...BLUEBERRY SKIN!

OMG, the sheer relief that went through us as we both gazed at it in the sunlight on the end of the spoon. I can't tell you the utter relief we both felt. I was so traumatised that I can't even recall what happened the rest of the day. Who knows if we actually went out or not; it was unimportant. What was important was that she was OK and this was the only thing that mattered. In that very short space of time, and for the first time as a human being (all thirty nine years of it at that time), I discovered the true fragility of life. It was a lesson I've not since forgotten, and I would suspect those of you reading this now may experience your own moments just like that one.

While I certainly hope you never do, I can say that far from being a bad experience it has made me only a better parent and all-round human being—at least in my own eyes. I've learned with this situation and with my time as a parent, that to experience the joys of children is certainly a challenging one. It is also one that is the most satisfying thing you could ever do. I really hope that like me, you can learn how important you are in your child's life and how vital your role is.

Circumstance may dictate that your role is not conventional, nor may it occur under the same roof with the other parent. However, these things don't matter as much when all that is important is that you are there, and are there for them. Play with them every day, read them stories every day, and make sure you listen to what they have to say. Really listen to them; they will know when you are not truly engaged in their conversation. Find the time because when it's done and dusted, you won't ever get the chance again and no amount of money or regret will ever bring it back for you. As our very wise Grandma often says as she gazes at our little ones; 'they really are a miracle'...and you know what? She's right.

Wishing you all the very best of luck on your journeys!

Tam, Louise, Lilly-Jo and Huey

ACKNOWLEDGEMENTS

I'm desperately trying not to go all "Gwyneth at the Oscars" here. However, trying to write this made me realise just how many people I have to thank. While I promise not to get too emotional, if you're on this list then you're either a very nice, or a very tolerant person, and I'm deeply indebted to you. This book was truly a family affair and couldn't have happened without my wife, Louise and my two children, Lilly-Josephine and Huey. Also my parents, Neal and Pam and brother, Telen, who were involved greatly in all manner of tasks that more often than not, involved getting bossed around by yours truly (Telen, here is your 15 minutes).

Then there are my amazing designers and editors: Maggie Meade, Kimberly Curran, Simone Hudson, Alyssa Thistlethwaite, Cain Lazenby, Gill Rapley, Diana West, and Andy Peterson, who did such an incredible job bringing my story to life.

Also to my friends: Stephanie Aldaz, Kawn Al-jabbouri, and Bridget Rodham, who were always enthusiastic and helpful, no matter how busy they were.

Special thanks to those people who helped me get into the position to write this book in the first place by supporting my business: Annabel Karmel, Ruth Yaron, Amy Roskelley, Natalie Monson, Richard Gallafent, Jennifer Stano, John Hayden Poole, Lindsey Laurain, Alexander Scott, Kerrie Dorman, Amy Morrison, Samantha Lear, Julie Heuer, Sam Skolnik, Natalie Brown, Rosie Nixon, Zahid Mahmood, and Matthew Trott.

Many thanks to both grandparents, Josephine and Larry.

Lastly, a sideways thank you to Ashton Kutcher and Ryan Reynolds for making diaper-changing cool. I salute you brothers!

Tam Rodwell

NOTES